THE NEW HUMANISM

THE NEW HUMANISM

ART IN A TIME OF CHANGE

BARRY SCHWARTZ

PRAEGER PUBLISHERS

NEW YORK · WASHINGTON

For Lynn,
who loves with me

Published in the United States of America in 1974
by Praeger Publishers, Inc.
111 Fourth Avenue, New York, N.Y. 10003, U.S.A.

© 1974 by Praeger Publishers, Inc.

Library of Congress Cataloging in Publication Data

Schwartz, Barry N
  The new humanism; art in a time of change.

  Bibliography: p.
  1. Art, Modern—20th century.   2. Humanism in art.
I. Title.
N6490.S334   709'.04   72–88674
ISBN 0–275–46640–0

Printed in the United States of America

CONTENTS

THE NEW HUMANISM

INTRODUCTION

I have written this book in order to bring to public attention the Humanist intention in art, especially as it has been realized in the work of many outstanding contemporary artists. I have pursued my goal by using two methods: rejecting current notions about art and its relationship to life, and searching for, and finding, art that is less visible than what is enthusiastically supported by galleries, art magazines, and museums.

While working my way out from under the pervasive assumptions of contemporary art history and criticism, I have rediscovered and redefined both old and new values and applied them in my analysis of twentieth-century art. I hope the reader will come to share my belief that my assumptions about art and life are themselves more valuable than the particular applications I have developed in this book.

My task here has been only to set right what has, for too long, remained a historical wrong. My passion, which may be occasionally rude to other art movements, is for Humanism in art. I believe that, unless we respond to its truths, we will be still less capable of a world that gives the highest priority to human needs. Although I may, at times, become enamored with my advocacy, I would want it understood at the outset that I have a love for all creativity. What is wrong with the world is not that we have too much of any kind of art.

I have not worked alone. Even in my solitude, I was able to draw upon the strength, conviction, and creativity of the hundreds of artists I met and the many more who corresponded with me. When I set out to write this book, I wrote a letter to artists that, in part, requested suggestions of other artists whose work I should see. The list grew geometrically. The stereotype of the artist as an alienated loner, contemptuous and competitive, proved to be unfounded. In general, I received help rather than cooperation; care and concern, rather than self-interested efforts.

The art presented here reflects only the art I was most able to respond to while the book was being written. The many excellent artists illustrated and discussed here are representative of the hundreds more whose work is important to me, who were helpful to me, but who, because of the limitations of one book, could not be given attention. To all of the artists, from many countries, who have assisted me, I extend my deepest gratitude. I hope I have proved worthy of their vision.

Regrettably, this book leaves much unsaid. My focus is on the visual arts; my interest is in the entire cultural domain. Perhaps the book will initiate greater discussion of the Humanist intention in all the arts, as well as draw some attention to the very significant community arts movement.

The New Humanism could not have been completed were it not for the creative assistance of Katherine Rosenbloom, whose devotion to the project was as great as my own. My first editor at Praeger, John Hochmann, shared my vision, and I am indebted to him. Cherene Holland, who transformed the manuscript into a finished book, has earned my admiration and respect forever. Finally, I owe thanks to the artists, the individuals who gave freely of their time, and the larger numbers whose contribution can never be adequately acknowledged.

THE HISTORICAL DILEMMA

Among the many attempts to explain why an early form of man decided, or felt compelled, to turn his spear into an implement for pictorializing his prey, the most plausible account is that the cave drawings manifested a belief in the magical powers of what we now call art. By naming, or visually rendering, the unknown—those things outside the control of man, those things that *are not human* —men felt less distant from the inexplicable. The Book of Genesis, for example, may be interpreted as the story of God's gift of language to man; a gift intended to provide man with the tools needed for the comprehension of his environment. This God, who leads Adam by the hand and gives him the words of the world is called *Adonoi*—the "unnameable one"— a fitting designation for a deity who, by definition, remained eternally unaffected by the powers of the human species.

From its origins, art was considered a form of magic. By magic, we do not necessarily mean supernatural power; we may mean only that the artist mediates between his powers of understanding and what cannot be understood. Thus, art is one way of enlarging the scope of the comprehensible environment. This view of art rests upon two assumptions: that man is sensitive to the unknown (that he is conscious, or wishes to be conscious, of it) and that the artist believes in his ability to respond to his environment. From the twentieth-century anthropological perspective, we see that the "magic" of early art was a rational endeavor—a crude but significant attempt to give meaning to those aspects of human experience that seemed terrible, absurd, or without explanation.

Western civilization is thought to have developed when man turned from magic to science, which is now believed to be a more sophisticated way of learning about the world. Science, in its earliest form— philosophical speculation—attempted to create cognitive order out of the world, while art "fixed" human experience in externalized forms. Such art, often without individual signature, provided a mythical representation, usually idealized, of both society and man himself.

Throughout early history, art and science were considered pursuits beneficial to the whole society. Although the human labor required to make art was often involuntary, art nevertheless affirmed the society that nurtured it. With the exception of Hellenistic art, which was a response to social crisis, harmonious relationships between art and society and between art and science remained intact from earliest times through the Renaissance.

Medieval society supported an art that reflected and affirmed the mentality and beliefs that those with social power desired to have expressed. Medieval art particularly encouraged the acceptance of the pervasive certitudes that characterized medieval life. Within a system of human structuring that allowed no deviation, that ordered all human behavior, medieval artists pictorialized and legitimized what was thought to be crucial to the stability of society. Theirs was a public art because the church was a public place. In the absence of any countercultural art, it was as much political in effect as it was religious in content. Art played an affirmative role, concretizing and elevating accepted truths.

We see here the longest stable system of human regulation that had ever existed in Western culture. It offered the individual one module within a totally organic construction. Man was secure, or at least as secure as he could be within a pretechnological environment. And man was not free. The Greek ideal of a harmonious balance between security and freedom (slaves excepted) was modified by the medieval world, which needed the death of freedom for the achievement of order.

The Crusades brought imaginative alternatives to the narrowly defined medieval world. The growth of small towns, then cities, created the possibility of mobility. With mobility came the dissolution of the family, a process that continues to this day. With the invention of the printing press came the potentiality of politics, the dissemination of knowledge, and separation of accusation and accuser. The introduction of a money system, movement to centers of population, the invention of the cannon, and the reintroduction of gun powder were fatal to the already vulnerable feudal system. With the rise of the middle class, capitalism, and the beginnings of industrialization came individuality, personal initiative, insecurity, estrangement, the collapse of communal life, and uncertainty in man's life, and, later, in his world. The Protestant Reformation ruptured theological certainty and articulated the spiritual questions modern man no longer has the patience to ask.

The collapse of the medieval world created freedom and confusion. The Renaissance was a time when everything was possible, when every philosophical persuasion, from exalted optimism to unrelenting pessimism, had a following. Like the present, it offered "Utopia or Oblivion"[1] as two extremes of the conflict between individual choice and social imperative.

Although his world view was dissolving, the Renaissance artist tried to achieve a synthesis of the diverse elements of human experience. The "Humanism" of Renaissance art was so named because of its varied anthropomorphic aspects. At a time when all values were in question, the Renaissance artist struggled to articulate his beliefs with conviction. While some tried to make the older values work, they knew that they could not achieve this goal unless previously dogmatic beliefs were incorporated within a human framework. The synthesis of both the spiritual and the temporal that we find in Giotto, for example, reflects the attempt to create an art that lives within the structures of a dying world, while remaining sensitive and receptive to the new.

Although the formalists of our time have admired Renaissance art primarily for its visual inventions, there remains a content to the art that, if not understood, neglects the liberated consciousness of the Renaissance artist. The Renaissance artist wished to bring together many aspects of his life, some old and some new, in an art that was, first for the artist and then for his fellow human beings, a communication of the subjective experience of living in this world.

Renaissance artists were the last to maintain effectively that art and science were complementary ways of knowing the world. The art of Leonardo, Dürer, Michelangelo, Grünewald, and Alberti was the last to engage questions of content and technical development without contradiction. But, however successful these particular artists may have been, we find, in the aftermath of the Renaissance, a growing tension between artists who admired the expanding influence of science and technology and those who were disturbed by its impact on human beings.

By the "Age of Enlightenment," society was already committed to the view that the "truths" of science, acquired through application of reason, would solve all human problems. The Heavenly City of the eighteenth century was to be constructed on human laws consistent with the laws of the universe. By the time Romanticism asserted itself as a cultural force, society had firmly committed its resources to the processes of nineteenth-century industrialism. Thus, the Enlightenment was a social reality and Romanticism was an artistic expression. By the middle of the nineteenth century, the boundaries of artistic turf had closed in, and art was still more narrowly defined.

No longer affirmative of society, now out of step with the thrust of social energies, the Romantic vainly tried to see nature again as an inexplicable and formidable force in the world. As an inverted metaphor for the loss of individuality concomitant with industrialization, Romantics posed human beings tragically but heroically pitted against the awesome forces of nature in revolt. But, however marvelous are the works of Delacroix, Gericault, Friedrich, and Blake, they could not convince a society preoccupied with machines, pavements, and products to rekindle awareness of nature. While the Romantics viewed nature as earth forces defying human presence (thereby elevating man to the heroic), nature itself submitted quietly to the manipulation of the tools of industry, finally to serve the frivolous and often destructive desires of mankind. Once the infinite container that held the world, nature is, today,

in the greatest centers of technological achievement, experienced only symbolically: animals in zoos and trees in parks. Nature is now collected.

For a metaphor of this historical process, we can look to Dante's Vergil as a symbol of rationality, and to Dante's Beatrice as the manifestation of divine intervention, including "magical art." When Dante wrote *The Inferno,* Vergil was able to lead the protagonist—and man—only so far. He could proceed no farther without the intervention of Beatrice. Since Dante's time, Vergil has been able to lead man farther and farther along the path until, today, many believe that Beatrice need not meet Dante at all. By the turn of this century, art was considered best served when unencumbered by the older requirement that it make the inexplicable known.

The crisis that marked the first two decades of the twentieth century was a crisis of identity. The human problems that had originated with the break-up of the medieval period threatened to envelop the world in a modern barbarism. Technological change was rapid, and society was allied to the technological myths: belief in progress, systems, states, collective optimism, organization, rationalism, function, and order. A re-evaluation of both the meaning and conventions of art and of the relationship between art and life took place as the crisis of modern life was felt throughout the culture.

Out of the confusion came two possibilities. Some artists chose to investigate the technological environment. Their exploration of the man-made world, paralleled scientific inquiry into materials, space, time, energy, architectonics, and the nature of perception itself. Other artists chose to oppose technological myths by creating a countercultural art. Generally, the opposition to the technological direction has been pessimistic, tragic, and concerned with liberation, injustice, individualism, and freedom (in the face of its denial).

The recent opposition to social "progress" first took the form of Dada, which was an expression of contempt. Dada was artistic noncooperation; the artist would no longer participate in the creation of illusions that diverted attention from reality. Dada was a statement of unconditional dissatisfaction: the artist's rejection of his own time. But Dada, though scandalous, was not an effective countercultural force. Marcel Duchamp complained, "I threw the bottle-rack and the urinal into their faces as a challenge and now they admire them for their aesthetic beauty."[2]

The last breath of Romanticism in art —Surrealism—tried to resurrect nature again as an inexplicable force. However, because Romanticism was driven into the human shell, nature had to be confined to the human psyche. Now nature was without a body; it consisted of spirit, of irrational forces, of the mysterious. Without an external reality beyond the mind of man, nature now needed man in order to exist.

The Romantic artist who wished to deal with society was required to do so only insofar as he investigated himself. The retreat of the artist into freedom in isolation was irreversible by the time Dada was already incorporated into art history; today, it is used to tell more about the artists involved than about the spiritual collapse of Western civilization. The technological track has continued, and the Romantic tradition has willed itself away in a dedicated but ineffectual protest against the modern world.

With the invention of the camera, a metaphor for the entire process of industrialization, many artists sought vitality by closing the distance between their art and the emerging technology. Impressionism was the first of a number of artistic movements to test the Romantic view of nature with a scientific one. It chose to explore light. Later, Cubism explored space and time. No longer believing in their "magical" powers, doubtful of their actual contribution, these artists participated in the general consolidation that was part of the larger technocratization movement. As was true in most other human pursuits, the artist began to think of himself as a specialist, a more imaginative form of technocrat, with dominion over a small part of the fragmented whole.

The idea of "art for art's sake," which differs dramatically from the idea of art for the species's sake, or even art for culture's sake, coincided with the artist's decision to leave to technology the human sphere of people, economics, and social and political relationships. Artists would now content themselves with discovery within those areas of human perception over which they thought they had some control. If they did so with enthusiasm, they were naïve, for scientific inquiry into natural processes would continue even into areas of visual perception, and further narrow the sphere of artistic activity.

Art became divided against itself as a result of the break-up of the medieval period; today, art is divided against itself as society moves toward a technological medievalism. In the modern stage of this historical process, since Dada and Surrealism, artists have had several versions of essentially two options: The first offers artists the possibility of paralleling or complementing science and the seemingly bold forces of technology, thereby playing a supportive role to the historical pattern, and affirming the direction of society; the second option is the human resistance to the blind technocratization of the human and natural environments. By no longer divorcing human life from modern life, this second option entails seeking a central role for art within the human situation. This critical perspective of the technological world is what Herbert Marcuse called the "Great Refusal."

The first option anticipates an *avant-garde* defined by its ability to innovate, discover, and change at a rate comparable with technological development; the second pictures an *avant-garde* based on the artist's ability to provide a countercultural force—an opposition to the acculturating forces that are part of the technocratization process. The first option has sometimes been characterized as modernism, but, whatever it is called, its primary identity is that it is a modern application of the theory of imitation. In this case, however, the imitation is that of the man-made environment. *Modernism is a technological portraiture.*[3]

The directions art has taken in the twentieth century reflect these two patterns.[4] The side of the coin seen in Impressionism, Post-Impressionism, Futurism, Cubism, Geometric Abstraction, Neoplasticism, Constructivism, Op Art, Minimalism, Pop Art,[5] and the New Abstraction all work toward finding the proper artistic mode, sufficiently unique while at the same time avoiding a tension between the dominant forces of technological change and the often brutal impact of these forces upon mankind. Modernism has remained aloof from subjective appraisals of modern life. Human resistance to the technological pattern takes the form of Surrealism, Expression-ism, Social Realism, and Humanism. This human resistance is characterized by the artist's willingness to risk, to oppose "the way things are," to provide cultural criticism, to help us see that optimism is a lie. If the modernist believes little is known and that he is about to discover, the artists who resist feel that much is known but too few are paying attention.

Throughout this century, there has existed an art that has expressed outrage at the castration of human life. It has often been lost in the shuffle of art movements, and its practitioners have usually been treated as eclectic creators. However, it is the critics and historians, not artists, who have failed to see that Humanism is a unique artistic intention. Unfortunately, the term "Humanism" has been frequently misused or soiled in discussions of art. It has sometimes been associated with a drab, academic, representational art. Further, artists of other persuasions have taken offense at the suggestion that their art is not equally "Humanistic." However much the word is embarrassing or cliché, I would still prefer to use it when describing the ever growing body of work created by living artists who share a common aesthetic. If this art is the cultural expression of the struggle to achieve new and credible values, a struggle that can be characterized as Humanistic, then it is appropriate to speak again of Humanism in art. It would be better, I think, to save a word, rather than take the advice of one curator, who urged me to "choose a catchy title" and "launch the new thing." Humanism in art is not the new thing.

Today we are encouraged to believe that art is indifferent or independent of so-called nonvisual values. The view that there should not be a social art in a time of social crisis is evidence of yet another way we are conditioned to police ourselves. Art historians and critics have usually refused to recognize and deal with the value orientation of Humanist art, perhaps believing, with the rest of society, that what is not recognized goes away. Humanist artists, themselves, have sometimes accepted, or pretended to have accepted, aesthetic theories that do little justice to their art. They have done this in the belief that it was required of them, if they were to survive as working artists, receiving recognition and exhibition. Some of the artists found in this book will be uneasy when labeled "Humanist," and discussed in the context of an intention that has previously been a private, not a public, expression of motivation. Obviously, Humanism has been affected by the crisis it communicates.

This crisis of modern life is inexplicable, beyond our reach, incomprehensible, and of enormous impact on human life. At a time of unparalleled potential for an environment that promotes the growth of healthy, fulfilled human beings, we live with distorted values, with war and nationalism, with the cruelties of empire-builders. Although disturbing social conditions have always existed, and artists have always responded to them, there has never been in the history of man another time symbolized by Dachau and Hiroshima. The people of the United States, the center of technological development, live with social fragmentation, polarization, poverty, racism, sexism, violence, ecological disaster and spiritual death. Values are built on lies, illusions, a pathological consumerism, and the evasion of what each person knows is true. Although the environment has been created in the name of satisfying human needs, the mechanisms of society are dehumanized, insensitive, and hopelessly beyond the reach of individual man.

Not simply a matter of political or social upheavals, today's crisis is the crisis of life itself. It is not alarms we hear; it is the roar of an apocalypse. At a time of greatest uncertainty, what scientists would call the point of maximum entropy generation, a time when men must choose between life and death, the Humanist believes, "The apocalyptic contingency must be recognized as *conceivable*, yet shown to be *avoidable*."[6]

Unable to account for the apocalypse by divine plan, modern man has no choice but to account for his actions as the realization of his identity. Rejection of present human action leads to the search for a new human identity, a new self-image of man in the world. The search for this new identity characterizes Humanism in life and in art. Unlike less critical tendencies, Humanist art tries to discredit technological myths with older and newer myths that prove human perceptions are as valid a guide for human behavior as are the systematized rules of conduct promulgated by the technological order. By opposing the direction of the society in which he creates, the Humanist artist is in a state of perpetual antagonism with reality. Out of this conflict comes his insight into what it is we need to know in order to be able to survive.

The Humanist will weigh and measure, evaluate and communicate those values that are seen to deny or encourage new ways for people to relate to the world and to each other. The Humanist insists on social change and participates in the creation of a system that offers greater sanity, humanity, and justice. But the demand for positive social change implies no illusion of its certainty.

The Humanist expresses both the desperation of the human situation and his own assertion of freedom. His images express the unacceptable, but, in his negation of past human choices, the Humanist affirms that men may live differently. The artist deals with the inexplicable, and he will be sensitive to all of the environment, even the most foreboding aspects of it. Humanist art is "magical." The nature that is the subject of Humanist art is human nature—what man does to man. Man is central to Humanist art because he is not now free, because Ivan Karamazov's vision of the Grand Inquisitor may be realized in the technological environment. We have been given "something that all would believe in,"[7] and, perhaps, we will soon be "led like a flock."[8]

Unlike the ethical philosopher who creates discourse, the Humanist artist creates a visual experience that, if successful, will stimulate the viewer's sensitivity to the reality of his human environment and the needs of human beings within it. The Humanist artist is concerned with life as it is experienced; he does not subscribe to the current fashion of separating logic from feeling, cognition from perception, feeling from intuition, and intuition from behavior. His art will generally be representational because his subject is explicit human experience and behavior, the forms of existence. However, the artist does not merely represent what is known, obvious, and enduring. He explores values and behavior within a context of confusion, pain, and crisis.

Humanism in art can be characterized by a commonality of interest and a shared intention realized in a diversity of styles and visual appearances. Yet, because critics have only been able to see connection between art works that *look alike,* they have characterized groups and movements solely on the basis of the formally similar qualities of a body of work. They have failed to develop a reasonable critique of the development of content in our time and have preferred, instead, to pretend that art history is the history of the progressive evolution of form. As a consequence, much twentieth-century art has been misrepresented.[9]

The inequities can be listed endlessly.[10] However, for our purposes, it is relevant to consider how art historians and critics have handled Abstract Expressionism. Today, the Abstract Expressionists are used to affirm American art generally and American formalism specifically. Referring to the "formalist writers on art, whose point of view came to dominate art criticism during the 1960's," Irving Sandler explains, "These writers narrowed their interpretation to formal problems, avoiding any analysis of content. Their underlying premise was that advanced artists conceived new styles by rejecting recently established styles that have become outworn through overuse."[11]

It is a bitter irony that, during the 1960's, an era that destroyed the lethargy of the previous decade by its energetic search for new values, art criticism was reduced to a preoccupation with style. Although Abstract Expressionism was motivated by humanist concerns and struggled to communicate content with integrity, the formalist critics have preferred to judge Abstract Expressionism as the artistic analogy to the scientific endeavor. They have, as Harold Rosenberg expressed it, engaged "in the systematic nibbling away of the meanings of Abstract Expressionist works through translating them into purely esthetic terms."[12]

The formalists refuse to acknowledge that Abstract Expressionism was a crucial holding action, a hesitation between the forces of technological development and the values promoted by human resistance to its most destructive impulses. Abstract Expressionism was a dedicated attempt to come to terms with the problems to be found at the boundary of two opposing sensibilities. Although the Abstract Expressionists could no longer perpetuate myths they felt to be untrue, they were unwilling or unable to lead the cultural opposition to the transformation of the environment.

Abstract Expressionism was, after all, a persona of lament—an expression of self and human presence through the experiences the artists believed were credible. Within the social milieu, at a time when brave men felt hopelessly confused and most men were no longer able to locate themselves, the Abstract Expressionists maintained human significance while avoiding direct confrontation with the dominant forces in the environment.

Sandler explains Abstract Expressionists this way: "Unwilling . . . to accept any other dogma, the Abstract Expressionists turned to their own private visions and insights in an anxious search for new values. The urgent need for meanings that felt truer to their experience gave rise to new ways of seeing—to formal innovations."[13] If the aim of the Abstract Expressionists was formal innovation, they were very successful. Indeed, they taught a whole generation—perhaps two—how to paint, if not how to draw. But, if their aim was to discover vital content, they were less successful and served only to keep human emotion legitimate at a time when it was forsaken elsewhere. Although the Abstract Expressionists objected to "geometric painting . . . based on their belief that it had become too much a matter of making pictures whose end was composition for its own sake,"[14] the criticism of the past decade imprisoned the Abstract Expressionists in the formalism they had opposed.

At the heart of Abstract Expressionism is the crisis of the individual. Abstract Expressionism kept a man alive, affirmed his human presence against the background of the machinery, but it did not fully anticipate the crisis of the species. The Humanist sensibilities in Abstract Expressionism took the form of an assertion of identity; Humanism today aspires to human connection—not identity, but relationship.

Abstract Expressionism was created while most of society was asleep—at a time when men valued careers, when the great American materialism was still a dream, when young people were radical because they swallowed goldfish, when Presidents were heard but not seen. It expressed as much content as could be credible after the failure of Social Realism. It was a movement directed by artists who experienced in isolation the crisis that would, in the 1960's envelop the entire society.

Unfortunately, the "battle" between abstraction and representational art has dwelled on unending exaggeration of their differences, ignoring the more substantial elements they sometimes have in common. The difference between the Abstract Expressionists and today's Humanists is not explained only by differing approaches to the making of art. Instead, what distinguish the two are the different ways artists impose limits on their subjectivity. The Abstract Expressionist confines subjectivity to the artist himself. The Humanist gives his own subjectivity an environmental quality. Thus, Abstract Expressionism embodies within the work the emotional life of the artist, whereas, in Humanism, we find the subjective experience of the species.

A transitional figure here is artist Willem de Kooning. The formalists, who wish to see only the innovative formal qualities of Abstract Expressionism, are frequently embarrassed by de Kooning's continual preoccupation with content. The emergence of the "woman" paintings, which are the continuing achievement of his art, moved de Kooning's art out of the realm of a highly personal idiom into a connective Humanism. De Kooning achieved content with integrity and developed a logical relationship, usually overlooked, between Abstract Expressionism and expressive representation.

The dilemma of content inherited by both Abstract Expressionists and Humanists can be traced to Social Realism, which, unfortunately, served to diminish the credibility of a countercultural art. If the art that affirmed the dominant directions of society supported the ideology of progress, Social Realism, which was antagonistic to the existing political system, allowed itself to succumb to similar myths. By subscribing to a "truth" that was not a truth but an ideological proposition, Social Realism blemished later attempts to create outside the swift stream of technological imitation. Although the "content" of Social Realism advocated change in the name of man, the illusions, myths, and faith of Social Realism were too similar to the decadent art to which it thought it was an alternative.

Social Realism did not maintain the tension between freedom and security that is necessary for the integrity of a Humanist art. Instead, it differed with modernist values only in terms of which conception of the eventually secure society history would prove to be accurate; historical inevitability was fundamental to both. The Social Realists denied freedom to the future in much the same way that the technological pattern affirms that,

despite ecological disaster and civil strife, dissent and polarization, the overall direction of society ("Progress is our most important product") is ensured.

Social Realist art, saddled with such imposing conceptions as proletarian revolution, caricatures of the ruling class, and repetitive images of the struggling worker, often lent itself to a political illustration that no longer worked. By offering its optimism as a counterbalance to technological optimism, Social Realism was as strongly influenced in its rejection of modernism as if it had followed the modernist tendency blindly.

The major objection that must be made to Social Realism is that, after a time, like the art it opposed, it became dishonest. It was not, of course, a form of realism at all. In its most vigorous expressions, it was actually a form of Surrealism. Its dream, however, was not the one that came with sleep but the one that came with history.

For the Social Realist, history was the insight of which one must be conscious. These remarks may be included as part of the standard rhetoric used to help ease Social Realism out of the history of American painting. But, if Social Realism failed as a countercultural mode, it was, after all, only an art that did not succeed. The blanket condemnation in our time of the art of the 1930's, and the fact that historical accounts of American art do not adequately deal with it, cannot be justified by Social Realism's failure to provide a viable artistic alternative to the art that has remained in vogue. Dada, too, was a failure, but we surely have reacted to the two in different ways—ways that support and follow the pattern of modernism.

Many of the Humanists discussed in this book have roots in the tradition of

Social Realism. But, unlike the Social Realists, these Humanists offer no view of historical inevitability. Today's Humanist is without dogma, without an encompassing ideology. Because he knows that the future is not predictable or certain, his work incorporates both the confusion and the possibility of our time.

Today, if art is to be political, it must be postideological. No ideology or spiritual formulation presently exists that does not have the potential for betraying the very mankind it says it wishes to serve. Although the Humanist may draw upon Social Realist art, he upholds human value against both the ideological collective and the corporate state. Still, the absence of ideology in Humanist art does not imply any diminution of the demand for social change. However, the social change envisioned—divorced from imposed labels—is simply a demand that people be able to be free, and live lives that are healthy, satisfying, and free of manipulation. Humanist art is created in the belief that there are no acceptable reasons why the resources and energies of man cannot now be directed toward the creation of a world free of the more grotesque aspects of contemporary life. It is political, insofar as it opposes those who would keep us from a new world by perpetuating the present one.

Yet, if Humanists are free of the illusion of historical determinism, the overall assumption that historical developments are *a priori* positive has been incorporated within the discipline of art history. Although the technological society wishes to maintain an appearance of progress, it abhors fundamental change. Contemporary criticism collaborates, freezes the moment, turns art into events. The Humanist is rejected because he is inherently critical of the present. By creating an art history that divorces art from its historical context, today's art historians and critics would have us believe that art has always been concerned primarily with its own conventions. Through a method of correlating styles and influences, these art professionals have pictured the history of art as being independent of the history of man. If art is truly a cultural phenomenon, the work of art must be seen related to its context. The critics and historians who speak about the universality of art, its ability to transcend circumstances, and to speak to all men and all time, in reality reduce art to a carcass that speaks to no man at any specific time.

Humanist art strives to be a cultural force. It wants to derive its authenticity according to the degree to which it is of this world. It is a constant reminder that the assumption of progress and the illusion of advancement are only conditioned reflexes within the technological environment; that if man suffers within the dehumanized environment, there will be an art that gives voice to his pain.

At times, the Humanist intention in art is ascribed to all artistic motivation. This is not correct, and describes only those artists who have refused to fit into and support technological optimism. Herbert Read, for example, demonstrates this confusion:

Art, on the other hand, is eternally disturbing, permanently revolutionary. It is so because the artist, in the degree of his greatness, always confronts the unknown, and what he brings back from the confrontation is a novelty, a new symbol, a new vision of life, the outer image of inward things. . . . The artist is what the Germans call *ein Rüttler,* an upsetter of the established order.[15]

Unfortunately, Read's wish that the artist upset the established order is not satisfied by many of those artists who are today very deliberate and calm in their ongoing neutrality and "professional" concerns. If they are capable of upsetting some small part of society, it is only because they, for the moment, are "news" —not because of their work, but because it is *their work.*

At this moment, there are at least as many artistic energies expended in affirmation of the established order as there are those against it. And, by upsetting the established order, I trust we mean specifically that art creates more than aesthetic controversy; we mean that it threatens existing structures.

On the other hand, what makes the established order secure are cultural structures that take the same form as societal structures. The art that today affirms the established order defines itself as a new profession, a specialization whose discoveries can be known only through its own enlightened discipline. It prefers to leave most citizens to their so-called popular culture, the fully programmed arm of the technological system.

As society moves towards completion of its technological task, it creates appropriate institutions for the arts. This has to be so. The technological society is not comfortable with a strong creative, unpredictable, and critical force within its midst that is not brought under influence or control.

As society has taken children out of the home to insure a more cohesive, uniform, and effective acculturation by placing them in schools, so, too, society has created vehicles in the form of enormous cultural apparatus to "educate" the artist. The continuing affiliation of artist with the university, the often disastrous intrusion of media and prominence into the lives of younger artists, the manipulation and support of museums as a way of emphasizing specific artistic directions, the use of foundation monies to pump prime the arts, the creation of a governmental bureaucratic arts management class— these are some of the factors that have assured that certain very general, very persuasive assumptions would continue to be made about art and the role of the artist in society. In a way that is perfectly consistent with the technological pattern, the arts are not controlled by overt political influence, but are "managed" by the "proper" means, which are support, access, and distribution. Those who express surprise at the fact that in our time the arts have become institutionalized and integrated within the mainstream of modern life are naïve, for society will accept the artist as long as his art is not *effectively* critical. The technological system within which we now live, like other systems offering regulation and security, harnesses the forces of culture to provide affirmation of the system.

Our society does not value the acknowledgement of the contemporary bison, the exploration and depiction of enigmatic and sometimes frightening realities. It values instead the continual discovery of things that can be known only through specific processes. The questions it likes to explore are dictated by the way it believes it can find answers. It encourages a pseudoscientific method that increasingly emphasizes methodology rather than value. As art has become integrated within society, and with the creation of the art marketplace, planned obsolescence has been built into art. The artist, in turn, has been redefined in ways that are consistent with the role of the professional, the specialization, and the marginal importance assigned to his endeavor.

We are living with what amounts to a *"science-centered curtailment* of human understanding."[16] As Edgar Wind has noted, many artists "seem to act in their studios as if they were in a laboratory, performing a series of controlled experiments in the hope of arriving at a valid scientific solution. And, when these astringent exercises are exhibited, they reduce the spectator to an observer who watches the artist's latest excursion with interest, but without vital participation."[17] The old is continually rejected for the new, like the processes of science itself, which affirm a method, but never claim any particular discovery to be of lasting importance. The turnover of new data is seen as a sign of the health of the process itself. Artists speak of color theory, serial painting, field painting, and other categories, based on a pseudoscientific exploration of visual experience.

Thus, modernism in art, the cultural analogue to the technological system, emulates science and technological innovation, and "proves" art to be a legitimate activity within the environment. I am reminded of Richard Anuszkiewicz's rationale for his art: "My work is of an experimental nature and has centered on an investigation into the effects of complementary colors of full intensity when juxtaposed and the optical changes that occur as a result."[18] In a similar fashion, artist Vasarely argues, "The masterpiece is no longer the concentration of all the qualities into *one* final object, but the creation of a *point-of-departure prototype,* having specific qualities, perfectible in progressive numbers."[19] Thus art is released with a countdown.

The formalism in aesthetics that is dominant in our time is rationalization for the continuation of an art that is compatible to the technological society. It is predictable that an aesthetic should emerge serving this "cleansing function." These aesthetic theories, which are only opinions with support, are what Marcuse has identified as "technological rationality." Not only do formalist aesthetics provide the context into which new art forms come and go, but it also provides a general rebuttal to Humanist arts.

Every artistic intention, and they are as varied as human choice itself, generates an aesthetic by which one is encouraged to understand the art and can choose to evaluate it. An aesthetic is, as Kenneth Clark put it, "a helpful background to art."[20] But, when the aesthetics of one intention is applied to another, as when the formalist aesthetic was applied to Humanism, we have a form of critical totalitarianism, in which individual works are rejected not because they are unsuccessful, but because what they intend to do is thought to be undesirable. As in all technological societies, the prevailing aesthetic today comes equipped with a set of "correct" values—in this case, valuelessness—"correct" intentions, "correct" ideology. The rules of the game are set up so that any art that does not make the preferred assumptions becomes rejected as "bad" art.

Though individual Humanist artists have, on occasion, passed the inspection of the critics, they have rarely been presented within the context of their actual intention. Because formalist aesthetics reject any attempt to bring what are thought of as nonaesthetic considerations to the work of art, the Humanist intention has been relegated to an obscure status. "Why," asked Clive Bell, "should artists bother about the fate of humanity?"[21]

The concern for human and social experience found in Humanist art antagonizes the formalists. In their attempt to create the rationale for modernism, and in their wish to neutralize countercultural forces in art, formalist critics have pretended that the judgments of art history are based on nearly scientific, objective criteria, and not on the cultural assumptions made by the critic himself. Although there is little hesitation among critics to use terms such as "bourgeois sentimentality," and "aristocratic frivolity," words which identify qualities of art satisfying the special requirements of a social grouping or class, critics have been more than reluctant to identify what, if any, grouping they respond to. Is this the job of later historians, or can we say now that much of modern criticism is based on "institutional compatibility"?

To articulate their bias in less vulgar terms, the formalists have employed the catch-all of all art discussion: the concept of purity. It is a very convenient term, for instead of having to say, "I don't like this," or "I find this offensive or disturbing," critics can now conveniently and authoritatively indicate that this or that work is "impure." It is only within the "rational" irrationality of our society that, in a time identified chiefly by war, ecological disaster, corruption, authoritarian ethics, credibility gaps, and the like, our art historians favor the notion of purity in art.

The contemporary fascination with the concept of purity is another borrowing from science. Within the scientific endeavor, there are two directions: applied science and "pure" research. Applied science is concerned with what science has learned only insofar as this "knowledge" can have an impact on the environment. Thus, applied science is infused with utilitarian values. Pure science is concerned with the continual discovery of what has not been previously known. The ideal of purity in art is analogous. Art that has messages, meanings, and utilitarian implications is impure, whereas art that leads along the path of formal inquiry and investigation of visual experience freed of all extra-aesthetic implications maintains its purity. Such formalist theories of art tend to regard Humanism, with its concerns for human values and social experience, as a misuse of art. Curiously, one sees overt hostility between pure science and applied science only when funding priorities emphasize one over the other. Perhaps, if the arts were as fully supported as the sciences, many of the "important" controversies in the arts would quickly be reduced to amicable disagreements over the "best" of artistic intentions.

Formalist aestheticians base their definition of purity on the view that painting and other arts must be concerned solely with so-called visual values, that subject matter, content, iconography, and even indirect representations of reality are either irrelevant to aesthetic experience, or destructive to the work of art. The purging of literary elements in the work of art is carried out against a straw man —the Renaissance Humanistic theory of painting, *Ut Pictura Poesis* ("as is painting so is poetry"). Not only have formalists misrepresented the actual theory itself, but they have also ignored the progressive changes that representational painting has undergone in centuries of development.

Though Read does caution us that "art criticism, even as an academic activity, has shown little consciousness of human psychology, and has remained a hazardous combination of subjective judgment and formal analysis,"[22] critics have steadfastly upheld an equation which, if universally accepted, spells doom not only for Humanist art, but also for much representation, generally: Modern representation equals older imitation equals very bad art.

The classic concept of imitation referred to art that was "an imitation of nature, by which they meant human nature, and human nature not as it is, but, in Aristotle's phrase, as it ought to be, 'raised'."[23] Renaissance Humanism expressed the ideal of human action and feeling in the face of a less than ideal reality; the contemporary Humanist expresses the *reality* of human action and feeling in the face of *its negation.*

The Humanist theory of painting assumed that art had to do with human life, the dignity of man, ideals or models of human behavior, and the expression of important emotions. If this theory were to be relevant today, it would have had to have undergone dramatic alteration. And it has. If the earlier Humanism saw, as one of its tasks, "to instruct mankind," this task is ever more complicated today, when men doubt the existence of truth, itself. If the Humanistic theory of painting wished to express serious emotions, the task of doing so has become infinitely more challenging in a time when men do not believe in their emotional lives. One cannot express the dignity of man easily in a time when human life and death are merely a matter of statistics. The Humanist today is clearly on the defensive. Human values are low on the list of social priorities. The Humanists may constitute a rear-guard action. Yet, in their attempt to disparage the Humanist concern, formalist critics have asserted that Humanism in art today is too easy!

Rather than deal with the philosophic problems of Humanism in our time, the formalists have ignored the problem of content entirely, and equated Humanism with a style and, more abstractly, with another art form, poetry, which they then claim nullifies the quality of the visual art created. Etienne Gilson, in *Painting and Reality,* describes the absolute position vis-à-vis Humanism when he writes: "A painting begins to become a book at the very moment it uses lines and colors to relate a story, or to describe human emotions, human passions, human thoughts —in short whatever could be as well expressed by means of words."[24] Herbert Read, in like fashion, insists that "human and spiritual values" have nothing to do with the aesthetic process itself.[25]

The formalists wish to establish visual art as its own discipline. They insist that a relationship between visual art and another art form is a betrayal of its true nature. Actually, they have substituted a relationship between art and music for one between art and literature. In doing so, they have also failed to see that contemporary Humanism, unlike *Ut Pictura Poesis,* relates not to poetry but to theater. While artists have every right to draw their aesthetic from the aesthetics of music, critics have no right to deny other artists legitimacy because they choose another aesthetic.

Humanism is an art of the dramatic. And, like all theater (I know of no exception), human beings are not chosen as subjects; if there is to be an experience, *they are required.* The attempt to lump all figurative art together is a refusal to recognize that certain figurative art, like the "new realism," is a formal approach to the visual object, whereas Humanism requires the human image not as a subject but as a presence through which subject matter is communicated. Even the pessimism of Beckett, the absurdity of lonesco, and the lament of De Ghelderode require human beings for the creation of the artistic experience.

Humanism incorporates Brecht's theatrical ideas of alienation. The "estrangement-effect" is designed to produce an experience in which the world can be recognized for what it is. "The experiences of everyday life are lifted out of the realm of the self-evident."[26] As Marx wrote, "Petrified conditions must be forced to dance by singing to them their own melody."[27] Humanist art will not be realized if the viewer filters out, or refuses to become involved with, experiences that are not pleasurable. You cannot ask Humanist art to make you feel good, to provide a playful and idyllic escape from depressing realities, or to assist you in finding relief from the painful experiences of your life.

With occasional exceptions, music is usually thought of as a strictly auditory experience. Though program music has had some prominence, the history of music is primarily an outgrowth of the history of musical composition. Visual art, which once tried to communicate some ideal beyond the strictly visual and sensuous, now is, according to the formalist, supposed to be to the eye what music is to the ear. From Impressionism to the present time, painting has borrowed from the vocabulary of music, but only certain music. Conceptual art, taken as a signal of the end of the object, is to painting what the compositions of John Cage are to conventional music. But who ever suggested that John Cage is the end of music?

In recent years, there has been created a new music and a new audience; a music of sounds and words, of auditory-sensory experience *and* compelling feeling. It is a music that is received by the ears of the young and the youthful; and, if analogies are to be made to music, we can say that Humanism in art is analogous to the music which affirms that sound and communication, rhythm and social experience, are not at odds with one another.

Yet another implication of the ideal of purity in art is the belief that consciousness is the enemy of creation. It is a position that is fully consistent with the technological orientation we are encouraged to inculcate. If individual consciousness is allowable, it would soon come into conflict with the tyranny of order and imposed stability. Instead, it is argued that art should be unrelated to the cognitive process—that, in Arnheim's words, "the areas of the mind farthest away from consciousness harbor the deepest wisdom."[28] Thus, consciousness is seen as an obstacle to art. Both the "rationalists," such as Kandinsky, Mondrian, and Gabo, and the "irrationalists," such as de Chirico, Breton, and Ernst, seem to have disagreed on everything except the notion that consciousness should be limited to the psyche, to the intuitive, and to the organization of inner phenomena. For Kandinsky, "the inner voice tells him [the artist] what he needs."[29] For de Chirico, the artist should feel "compelled to paint . . . by an impulse even more urgent than the hungry desperation which drives a man to tearing at a piece of bread like a savage beast."[30] Such views obviously promote both frenzied automatism and cognitive detachment in art. Painting should not involve thought, deliberation, conception, and willful intention.[31]

The more recent formulations of the ideal of purity do not allow even the inner world of the artist. For example, artist/theoretican Ad Reinhardt argues that

"The first rule and absolute standard of fine art, and painting, which is the highest and freest art, is the purity of it. The more uses, relations and 'additions' a painting has, the less pure it is. . . . The less an artist thinks in nonartistic terms, and the less he exploits the easy, common skills, the more of an artist he is. 'The less an artist obtrudes himself in his painting, the purer and clearer his aims.' The less exposed a painting is to a chance public, the better."[32]

The concept of purity in art, the emphasis on the intuitive and nonconscious approach to creation, the disappearance of the artistic self, the rejection of consciousness, the pseudoscientific definition of the art professional, and formalist aesthetics, have all attempted a *fait accompli*—the impossibility of a strong and vigorous challenge to modernism by Humanist artists. The alternative to this academic conception of art is to be found within the Humanist intention, which strives to be integrative and holistic.

Some art historians and critics are so remote from the major questions involved in content that they have lumped all representational art together, and have failed to develop an intelligent critique of the differences between the many kinds of figurative art now created. In recent days, an art has emerged which has been heralded as "a return to the figure."[33] This new figuration claims to take nature as it is. The artist's stance is conspicuously cool, detached, and uncommitted. "Realists," like Philip Pearlstein, insist that their art makes no judgments, offers no human involvement beyond the eye itself. In his wish to dissociate himself from any implications beyond the purely visual, Pearlstein turns the human subject or human presence into an anatomical object under the scrutiny of visual perception (*See Ill. 1*). He has argued that his model is of no more interest than the furniture she sits on. Unfortunately, the critics who have welcomed Pearlstein's "radical realism" have forgotten that many artists have never left the figure, and, therefore, they could not "return" to it.

Though the realists would like to be known, in Jack Beal's words, as "struggling Humanists," they, in fact, are generally cautious painters. They exist between two worlds—between loyalty to conventional notions of form, and a full-blown investigation of content. The new figurative art makes no value judgments. It claims to be an art of perception. But to perceive the human figure and to make no judgments about it, in the face of contemporary experience, is to make a significant judgment about it. The cultural domain of the technological environment requires that artists strive for acceptance on the basis that their work is free of values. Today, success requires the artist to hide behind his retina.

The critics will approve of the use of the figure, as long as there are no implications associated with its use, as long as the artist makes no unaesthetic judgments. The acceptable figure is reduced to merely another object available for sensual and visual investigation. If the artist's wish is to depict nature, his *danger* is that he evaluates it.

In contrast to this new realism is Humanism, a form of empathetic figuration which requires the figure, but never solely as form. Humanism distinguishes itself from generally figurative art by the artist's conscious decision to judge, to permit self-disclosure. Unlike formalist art, abstract or figurative, Humanism sees beyond the face into the life of the person. It illuminates what other artistic intentions help us to hide. The present figuration would pretend to deal with surface realities of vision without evaluating what it is we see. At a time when society is fragmented and torn by mechanistic violence; at a time when two out of every three hospital beds are filled with the mentally ill; at a time when nature herself is dying the ecological death, the formalists would divorce the eye from the brain. If, in art, we cannot deal with our feelings, our maladies, our sicknesses, how will we ever find a vision of health?

Some argue that the new realists are pioneers, that they are responsible for making a viable figurative art in our time.

But, we must ask, "For whom are they making it viable?" Clearly, within the narrow confines of the art profession, the new figuration is a pioneering attempt; but, from the point of view that goes beyond the closed circle of art-world assumptions, these "pioneers" are only in-house radicals. Given the long-standing commitment of Humanists to the image of man, placing a figure on the canvas does not appear as an awesome achievement. What makes the new realism different from Humanism in art is that the Humanist is committed to the intention, while the realist defines the boundary of his effort by that point where the art world begins to complain.

1. Philip Pearlstein, *Nude on Orange and Tan Drape,* 1967. Oil on canvas, 44″ x 50″. Courtesy Allan Frumkin Gallery, New York.

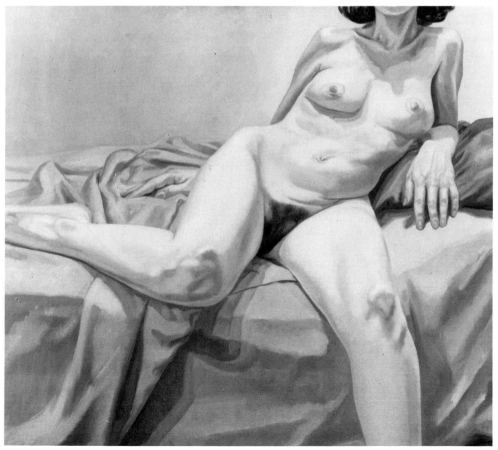

The realists do create tension and silence in their works—a tentative statement of crisis. By slowing down the motion of life, by stopping time and holding space, they give dignity to what would otherwise pass in the stream of events. But, where the "radical" realist creates tension, the Humanist creates crisis.

In all probability, the new realism will generate its alloted number of critical articles, shows, and books. It will be "discovered," promoted, reach its apex, and be replaced by the next artistic novelty occupying our attention. If it finds a value orientation, it will acquire endurance. If it does not, it will have been a passing formal figuration that created some interesting works, a lot of camp followers, and turned on a few realists to the Humanist aesthetic.

Clement Greenberg wrote, in 1944, "Let painting confine itself to the disposition pure and simple of color and line, and not intrigue us by associations with things we can experience more authentically elsewhere."[34] Insofar as the new realism politely disagrees with Greenberg's proclamation, some three decades later, the new realism is "radical." But, if some new realists have disagreed with the formalists' insistences, the modernist tendency has followed them with undistracted dedication.

In the aftermath of Abstract Expressionism came a "new" abstraction devoid of all concern with value and content. Stella, Noland, Olitski, and Louis created an art object that was not, as Read put it, symbolic, but only purely visual. Action painting transformed the object into the trace of a process. All that followed —Minimalism, Op Art, Pop Art, Kinetic Art, etc.—embodied in some form contempt for the holistic view of art. Finally, conceptual art wishes to do away with objects entirely. Is it altogether surprising that sophistication of the formalist aesthetic leads to the rejection of the art object?

I don't think so. Formalism in art has served as the technological ideology in the cultural domain. When it wished to discount a countercultural art, it claimed it was literary. When it wished to praise the works of Robert Indiana, Rauschenberg, Johns, Lichtenstein, and Rivers, it did so because they were literary, because they were "combined with poetry."[35]

Such inconsistencies are explained by the fact that formalist aesthetics over the past decade substituted inventiveness for impact. The emphasis shifted from the artist's creation to the originality in the doing or making. Kenneth Noland is known as a great colorist, not because of the subtlety and variation of color that are found in his work, but because of the original way the painter *uses* color. While the formalists have insisted that art is a purely visual experience, their enthusiasm has often been for the concept realized in the work.

"If a man," wrote Marcel Duchamp, "takes fifty Campbell Soup cans and puts them on a canvas, it is not the retinal image which concerns us. What interests us is the concept that wants to put fifty Campbell Soup cans on a canvas."[36] And Duchamp should know. When we see a Roy Lichtenstein painting of Mickey Mouse, do we become involved visually in seeing the comic character, or are we not delighted by the fact that we admire the artist's *idea* of turning a comic strip into an aesthetic object?

Yet, when an artist puts a political message in his art, which is merely another concept, critics are quick to relegate the work to the inferior status of a "political painting," and a misuse of visual experience. If we get past the rhetoric, we see that the critics are affirming one literary idea (invention) over another (social consciousness), and that their criticism is as ideological in its basis as if it were a criticism based on political theory. A political idea is still, after all, an idea. The "objective" standards of formalist art criticism are based on the assumption that one set of ideas is better than another. This attitude perpetuates an environment that sees the expression of morality as politics, and politics as bad art.

The art that affirms the technological direction of society has, in recent days, become less distinguishable from the technology itself. For creation, some artists have substituted manufacture. In place of consciousness, they have preferred accident or impersonal repetitive imagery. The patron who purchases a Warhol does not purchase an object—he buys "a franchise in a certain mode of existence."[37] The technological aspects of contemporary art production have led many to conclude that the manner by which works are created implies great significance. Edward Lucie-Smith writes that "the banal patterns of Johns, the inert canvases of the color painters, the light hypnosis induced by op, the blankness of Tony Smith's cubes: all of these might be seen as devices through which we unfocus, and become passively open to the world."[38] Others argue that the aridity of much contemporary art is itself a statement about the alienation of modern man. It is said, for example, that Pop Art is critical of existing society; that Andy Warhol's soup cans and Claes Oldenburg's soft objects are fundamental put-downs of society. Here the critics forget to distinguish between the sign of an experience and the experience symbolized. As Suzanne Langer points out: "A natural sign . . . is a *symptom* of a state of affairs . . .[39] symbols are not proxy for their objects, but are *vehicles*."[40] In other words, the fact that some neo-Dada and Pop Art *refer* to the crisis of our time does not mean that they are committed to the symbolic exploration of it. The symptomatic aspect of recent modernist works reveals the union of art and commerce. Works are increasingly worth less for themselves and more as documentation of the signature of the artist. Within the modernist aesthetic, art is no longer useless; it now serves a product function.

It is not revolutionary to do away with the art object. It is being done away with in all sectors. Not a mighty blow to the art establishment, the primary effect of this act will be to make it possible for collectors not only to collect art but also to collect artists.

Humanists refuse to give over to the mass media images which require a value context, that require not only observation but also response. In contrast to the impersonal mass media image, Humanists use their own hands and the hand-pulled print to place the information of the world in a context for evaluation. Though their attempt to resee images that flash by us may not be effective against the onslaught of the media, from a cultural point of view, they represent the struggle of individual man for life in the collective society.

The Humanist searches for a cohesive vision that will make it possible for men to live in community. But we are no longer innocent. We do not embrace spiritual endeavors with enthusiasm. Thus, Humanism is a search for myth in a desert of disbelief.

THE HUMANIST INTENTION

. . . a myth is a way of saying something about yourself, something that other people could understand and would be better than us, more beautiful, it wouldn't hurt me so much to tell it that way.

> —LOUIS, a boy of eleven, quoted in *Teaching the "Unteachable"* by Herbert R. Kohl.[41]

A scientific world does not lend itself to dreaming and to doubt. Instead, it prides itself on analysis, logic, and ordered processes. Civilized man believes he no longer dreams the collective dream that is myth. He forgets that the technological society itself is constructed on myth.

Statistics, "scientific proof," the "rationality" of institutional life, "corporate philosophy," "Bombs for Peace," and "weapons for defense" are contingent on myths of science and technology that support belief in optimism, perfectibility, and evolutionary progress. These technological myths are the target of Humanist art, which seeks to replace the illusions of well-being with icons of discontent. As it can be argued that the fall of the Roman Empire was inevitable partly because the myths of peace, which were so popular at its end, came too late, so it could be said today that, unless we break out of the mythical framework of the technological embrace, we, too, will be doomed. We have need of an alternative reference, one that transforms our self-image from efficient functionaries to pained and joyless victims of a system out of control. Only by dealing with what we have become can we redefine our goals, and create a destiny worthy of the twenty-first century.

Louis, the eleven-year-old in Herbert Kohl's classroom, knows myths are about ourselves; they express reality in a way that helps us comprehend what otherwise might be too threatening to be acknowledged.

While the modernist has shown us much about the technological transformation of society, he has done little to reveal the impact of this transformation on human life. Humanism in art responds to the impact of technological change on the quality of living; an impact that has, to paraphrase Camus, made the world unclear. We have need of an art that attempts to clarify. Myth-making art is art "magic."

A myth communicates something about ourselves. Humanist myths communicate a vision of what the artist thinks and feels we have become. Unfortunately, the Humanist's wish to communicate has been all but ruled out of aesthetic discussion. The formalists have wanted only to perceive art through the formal tools of analysis or by the requirements of the marketplace. Critics and art historians alike have remained unwilling or unable to contact, feel, and describe the communication of the art work. They have supported this neglect by asserting that the painter's experience with the work is solely important, and that the viewer's experience with art is only of minor interest.

The refusal of formalists to deal with the experiences of those outside the closed world of art invention is typical of the contemporary elitism found among other technocrats in the technological environment. This refusal implies that art experience is not, in fact, intended to communicate to the average person, but only to those already initiated into the profession's visual literacy. Like technocrats and bureaucrats, the artist and the critic are encouraged to achieve status by showing how many shares (training, education, apprenticeship, connections) of the cultural knowledge bank they hold. Fortunately, a work of art does poorly as an interoffice memorandum.

A work of art comes to exist through the artist's being—sensory, intellectual, subconscious, and emotional perceptions. It is a thing of paint, of color, of form, of texture, of smell, of time and space, of a thousand sensory impacts occurring simultaneously. The work of art may or may not be preconceived, but it is always a surprise. It is all of these things for the painter; the painter's experience with the object is really not with the object *qua* object at all, but with the process through which the object is created. The painter or printmaker discovers, grows, creates, and finds things he or she did not know were there. Out of the infinity of possibilities that exist on any blank canvas or unscored plate, a definite specific visual experience is created.

But there is more than the painter to be considered; it is here that we part company with formalist aesthetics. There is an "other"—the nonmaker. And though the artist may or may not create with this "other" in mind, once the work is completed, it belongs as much to the "other" as it does to the artist. I think this is what Mark Rothko meant when he said, "The instant one [painting] is completed, the intimacy between the creation and the creator is ended."[42]

The "other" is unable, though he may, and should, try to locate himself fully in the process by which the work was created. Consequently, the "other" must come to terms with the work itself, *qua* object. He must deal with the "ends" of the process. Not to respect the special problems and/or talents and/or contributions of the "other" to the painting is to say that paintings are for painters—which, I think, some of us do not want to say.

The "other" will engage in a new process in many ways opposite to the processes of the artist. Where the artist started with nothing (nothing fixed or definite) and created a new experience in the world, the "other" is presented with an experience that is everything to him. The sensuality, the emotion, the meaning, the impact he feels—all are to be found within a confrontation with the object. The "other" is given a thing which is "fixed," filled, done. At first, it is more than he can see, more than he can feel, more than he can understand. His problem is not to create something out of nothing; he must comprehend, absorb, and perceive something which at first seems monumentally alien to him. While the painter must bring to the canvas numerous emotions and perceptions in order to create the work, the "other" must contact his emotions, his feelings, his experiences, his sensitivities in order to maximize his experience with the work of art. If this were not the case, the painting would be merely another stimulus inducing an automatic response; the behaviorists would be correct in thinking that we *can* control human emotions by learning specifically which stimuli create which specific responses.

The "other" is not a passive spectator, not a yea-sayer to the visual truth. Nor could he be. The work of art is not "clear"; it is a mystery. One has to live with art a very long time before one perceives the dimensions of that mystery.

Still, the "other" is compelled to seek a communication. First, this communication is purely visual: I see. Colors exist, textures appeal, lines suggest, and so forth. Forms are pleasing or disturbing. Brush strokes are bold and vigorous, or hidden and muted. After a time, the "other" will become visually familiar with the work. He will go deeper, past, through. Though never outside the visual experience, the "other" contacts the artist, seeks to know his vision, his emotions. Summoning sensitivity and awareness, the "other" will enter the essential nature of the thing that is before him.

The relationship between artist and viewer is one outstanding aspect of the holistic aspiration of Humanist art. The Humanist artist needs the viewer for completion. Since the work strives for human connection with the viewer, since the symbolic and mythic orientation of the work is useless without viewer engagement, the Humanist, perhaps more than others, has the viewer centrally in mind while he creates his work.

The Humanist intention in art is evident explicitly within the work, and does not lend itself to revision and avoidance. The realities of contemporary existence are not implied by, or to be deduced from, Humanist art, but remain embedded in the work's visual reality. What can one say after seeing Kienholz's *The Illegal Operation* (*Ill. 2*)? How easy is it to enter into academic discussions on environmental sculpture? How many critics are able or willing to reveal the emotions they feel when they see this work? How much guesswork is necessary for one to conclude that the artist did not create this work in order to initiate a discussion about *art*?

The condition of man is not to be analyzed from Humanist work—it is found in the experience of the work itself. Effectiveness, for the Humanist, is not found in the critic's judgment, but in the viewer's emotions, which are coerced, induced, urged, stimulated, and provoked. Unfortunately, formalist writers have forsaken the experience of the "other." Consequently, they have never developed the visual and mythical vocabulary of Humanist art. Their decision to avoid the artist's communication is based on a conception, an idea, a value, about the role of art. Within the technological system, we are supposed to accept blindly the belief that art is only something to be looked at, a retinal experience, exclusively.

I think Kenneth Clark has summed up the present situation:

We now believe [art] should aim at producing a kind of exalted happiness; this really means that art becomes an end in itself. Now it is an incontrovertible fact of history that the greatest art has always been *about* something, a means of communicating some truth which is assumed to be more important than the art itself. The truths which art has been able to communicate have been a kind which could not have been put in any other way. They have been ultimate truths, stated symbolically.[43]

Why is art valued in our time? To decorate? To be beautiful? To entertain? To solve "visual problems" posed by "visual people"? Unfortunately, the present patronage of art desires little more. And, surely, where there is a market for art, there will be art to fulfill the needs of that market. But the Humanist today is not hoping to be decorative or entertaining. Nor is the Humanist motivated solely by the solution of visual problems. Though he will, like his fellow artists, strive to create a visual experience that is satisfy-

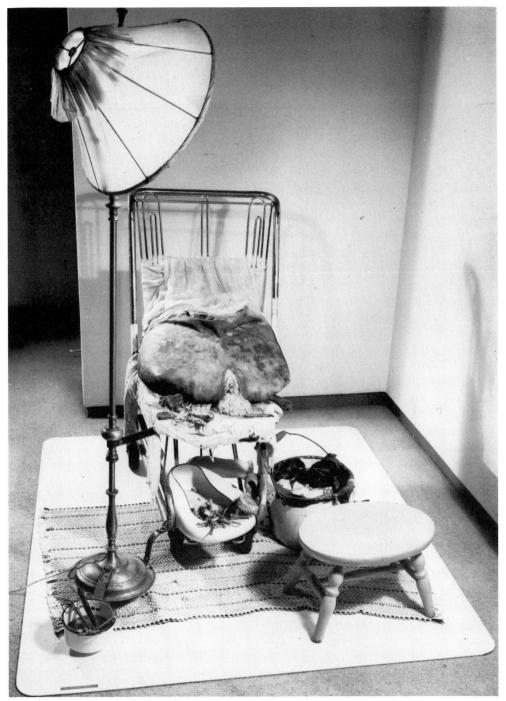

2. Edward Kienholz, *The Illegal Operation,* 1962. Mixed media, 59″ x 48″ x 54″. Collection Mr. and Mrs. Monte Factor.

ing on all levels, an experience that works, he is neither solidly committed to the consumer product art world nor to the Platonic ideal of beauty. I would suppose that, if anything, the Humanist is concerned with what Clark called "communicating some truth."

Unfortunately, we live in an age of disbelief. We interpret beliefs as merely psychological mechanisms for securing wants, needs, and desires. In this environment, truth is reduced to opinion, and the truth-seeker is regarded as naïve, insincere, or foolish. In response to the pervasive disbelief of society, many have felt it necessary to assume absolute positions in order to draw attention to their convictions. There are those among us who argue that only certain specific truths exist: ideological truths, religious truths, class truths, happiness truths, or trip truths. The distinguishing feature of the Humanist is his wish to communicate his beliefs, thereby opposing the relativity within the environment, but without dogma and self-righteousness.

If belief is to be credible today, it must contain contradictions. Man's actuality is a truth, but so is his possibility. By its nature, then, Humanist art will exist as an enigmatic statement of beauty and horror, of order and chaos, of diminishment and potential stature, of possible nobility and a now fallen state. Humanism is an art which presents the psychological and physical realities of life within the Western technological environment, while, at the same time, expressing that this state is a matter of fact—not of necessity. I think of number 42 of Goya's *Caprichos* which pictures asses on the backs of men, and the inscription, "They Cannot Help It." The men believe there is nothing to be done but carry them. Thus, the absurdities of modern life and its conflicts

are presented as the choices of men, not as the requirements of history. Humanism is tension-filled art that provokes us with what we would not wish to see. It is not popular; it is often not acceptable; it is often not sufficiently pretty; but it is most appropriate.

If Humanist art is to be successful, it must offer the possibility of involvement. If the work is mild, familiar, or trite, if it bores or disinterests the viewer, then the artist had better reconsider his objectives. Humanist art stands for a commitment to communication; and, if it lacks force, it quickly falls into a less ambitious, figurative art. The viewer will become involved when the art is authentic, when it pushes against boundaries, when it refuses to opt for easy solutions. Although the same can be said for all successful art, the special problems involved in exploring content require the Humanist artist to develop both content and formal solutions in the work.

The Humanist believes that one must see a metaphorical death before one can imagine rebirth. The greater the intensity of the work, the greater its capacity to erode the defenses (psychic and visual) erected by people who wish not to see what the Humanist feels they need to see. Because Humanist art wishes no longer to be marginal, because the artist tries to be more than a "professional," Humanism requires a relationship between the artist's life and his work. Unlike many artists today, who have much to say about the human condition in interviews, but who avoid contaminating their work by such concerns, the Humanist tries to integrate his life and his work. The work becomes an extension of the artist. When this is not the case, the work tends to lack vitality, to be more formalized and less authentic. Humanist art, for these reasons, is far more autobiographical than are the modernist experiments, which encourage the greatest distance between the artist's life and his work.

Certain artists, critics, and art historians will look at some of this work and remark that "it is the same old thing." But for whom is it "the same old thing"? American Social Realism is unknown to the generation that grew up admiring the old masters of Abstract Expressionism. Humanism, indeed, Social Realism, is for this new generation like a vision—unthinkable, unseen, and worthwhile. Many contemporary Humanist works are rejected as part of the larger objection to Social Realism, in the name of protecting an audience that has never seen the works of the 1930's.

The singular vision of today's Humanist is primarily his own. To say that a Humanist work is the same old thing is little different from looking at contemporary photography and rejecting it because photographers employed human beings as subjects in past photography. Convenient. The critics mistake Humanism for a style, and then reject it because it is an old style. Rarely would this logic be applied in any other artistic intention.

Unlike most figurative artists, the Humanist takes a stand. He interprets what he sees, and his interpretation is as vital to the work as the thing seen. The Humanist affirms emotional lives at a time when emotion is seen as a hindrance to successful functioning. By its very nature, then, Humanism is the insistence that from actuality something better must emerge. Through a rejection of what men have come to regard as normal, the Humanist creates the avenue for acceptance of new values. As he identifies the realities of our time, its illusions, its slogans, its programed human relationships, and

its lies, the Humanist creates his own mythical base, which recognizes both the limitations of the human condition and the need for a more acceptable social condition. In this sense, the Humanist adds to the existentialist: If God is dead, everything is allowable—yes, but not everything is preferable. What gives man his spiritual dimension is precisely this ability to make choices.

Some Humanists wish to create a history of our time. Without statistics and ideological historical accounts, they present images that identify life essentially as it is lived. All the artists presented here share the equality that Lawrence Alloway attributes to the work of Francis Bacon: "The violent or provocative nature of the image turned us, as we looked, into involuntary witnesses."[44] Humanist art disturbs, so that a human reality can exist that is more satisfying and less destructive. To this end, the Humanist values the integration of faculties, of mind and body, of intelligence and emotion, of art and society, of human experience and man's expression of it. There is a wish for wholeness in a time of fragmentation. This imaginative defiance of the technological order is expressed visually in satirical, philosophical, political, and tragic modes.

The final attempt of critics to undermine Humanist art is usually based on an artistic analogue to what in literary circles is known as "The Intentional Fallacy." This argument holds that the artist's intention is irrelevant to the interpretation and evaluation of the work. There is no reason, it is argued, to presume that the artist actually created an object consistent with his intention. Quite so. But perhaps we should quickly invent another argument: "The Critical Fallacy." This view holds that it is equally erroneous for a critic to evaluate and discuss art with a view toward what the critic thinks the art *should have intended.* There are innumerable examples of this critical treatment of Humanist art; some are presented in this book.

The fact that the formalist critics' assumptions about art are different from those of the Humanists may be taken only as a difference of opinion, and not as a rationale for the denigration of a particular artistic intention. Certain critics and art historians believe that viewers must be trained to see, that seeing is a learned discipline. But one could equally argue that critics have to be trained to feel, that most art history and art criticism, in their pseudoscientific guises, have long ceased to engage the work of art. Critics and art historians categorize, debate the worth of manifestos, place the work in chronological perspective, and characterize its influences. While they speedily place the newest art form within the purview of twentieth-century art, they often do not feel, or react, or let us know, what it is like to have an experience with a work of art.

Because the Humanist sees the crisis of our times not as personal *angst,* but as human and social conditions that he is compelled to communicate about, and to create awareness of, his work is filled with the signs and strains of our time. What Humanists see as essential awarenesses, without which the quality of life will be greatly diminished, formalist critics persist in seeing as corruptions of the work of art. What Humanists create as sometimes archetypal, sometimes concrete, images of our time, critics dismiss as images that are too ugly to be acceptable within a proper, tasteful modern art.

Typical criticism of Humanist art confuses the beautiful with the pretty. For example, a crucifixion in and of itself is not beautiful. It is a visual representation of a man dying, tortured, and bleeding. From one viewpoint, it is one of the goriest subjects of Western art. Yet critics find most of the painting of the medieval and Renaissance periods, with their crucifixions, beautiful or very acceptable. Why? The answer is that *the context* of the work is mythical, and suggests that, though the images may seem distasteful, the nature of the myth is positive and affirmative. The same may be said, but usually is not, of secular crucifixions. Though the images may be distorted or painful, the visual appearance does not determine the beauty of the thing—the symbolic content does. The Humanist believes the recognition of these images and their reality is a life-affirming act, without which man will continue to participate in the drive to death. Beauty is a matter of understanding, depth, and profundity that goes deeper than the visual impact of the image on the retina. By beauty, the critics today often mean optimistic, playful, undisturbing, free of demands, nice, and so forth. Unless the critic or art historian accepts Humanist assumptions, at least for as long as he looks at Humanist work, he will be unable to deal with this art. If he is attuned only to the artist who puts us at ease, who would have us appreciate his form, color field, and experimental direction, the critic or historian will fail to understand those artists who tell us that complacency is a more passive form of suicide.

In future years, the formalist aesthetic will undergo revision. When this particular aesthetic is revised, modified, or rejected, we will *then* see how many works of art were misunderstood or not understood because the prevailing aesthetic was not able to deal with them. Though the Humanists vary a great deal in terms of how well they achieve their shared intention, I will leave it to others to demonstrate which are the better. My wish here is to develop an understanding of the Humanist intention, and to present works which incarnate the vitality of Humanist creation in our time.

To this end, it is helpful, though not always accurate, to categorize Humanist art by the artist's stance toward the crisis of modern life. The emotional stance of the artist is what finally gives the work its characteristic form. Some Humanists see the present as one point on the continuum of tragic human existence. These artists lament our particular condition. They are metaphysical in their concerns, and mythical in their mode. Other Humanists are angered by the destruction and spiritual bankruptcy, and create images of diminished man as existential statements of human identity. Other Humanists are angered by the social conditions. Their art will be explicitly political, the expression of the imperative of change. Still other Humanists investigate human lives, and create a contemporary portraiture. And, finally, there are Humanists who wish to smash the belief that what we usually regard as normal is healthy and sane. These absurdists reveal the fundamental irrationality of programmed human behavior.

The stance of the artist determines the way he chooses to explore content. The metaphysical Humanist creates work that is active symbolically; he engages the viewer in the interpretation of the work. The existential Humanist creates images that confront the viewer by provoking a response. The absurdists employ a repulsion-curiosity mechanism: The viewer is repelled by these parodies, but, as it is human nature to do so, comes back for many more curious looks. In the end, he is led into a re-examination of his value system, or, if he is among the initiated, he is lead into a form of humor that takes delight in the exposure of modern madness. The political Humanist wants to contact the viewer's feelings of oppression and struggle.[45]

Whatever form it takes, all Humanism embodies a tension between life as it is lived and life as it could be lived. The dual vision of the artists is comprised of views of man both as a creature worthy of admiration and as the victim of contemporary experience. The Humanist aesthetic is best demonstrated when the totality of human experience is maximized by this tension between human potential and human actuality. If the work expresses only human potential, it becomes an ineffective form of romantic protest, a fantasy unconnected with life as it is lived. If the work contains only actuality, it reverts to a crass realism that goes no farther than the human eye.

However the Humanists vary in the ways they achieve their art, they hold in common and validate a Humanist aesthetic motivated by the priority of human life, the necessity of change, and their willingness to contribute to the possibility.

THE REALIZATION OF THE HUMANIST INTENTION

Metaphysical Humanism: The Search for Essence

An expression of hope and lament, metaphysical Humanism communicates its truths through icons symbolizing the crisis of contemporary experience. The metaphysical Humanist wants to distill from the social context the ultimate significance of our condition. By assuming a philosophic stance, the metaphysical Humanist aspires toward an overview, a broadness of vision, an essential metaphor for man's struggle to achieve dignity, meaning, beauty, love, and justice.

The metaphysical Humanist communicates a perception of reality infused with poetic or lyrical qualities derived from his inherent respect for the human being. The men and women within the world of the canvas or print are involved in human crisis; but the atmosphere of the work, these frozen moments of history, and these images of eternal solemnity, are themselves reassuring. Unlike many of his fellow Humanists, the metaphysical Humanist will not debase the figure as a way of communicating society's debasement of man. Thus, in metaphysical Humanism, we have a unique vision encompassing the crisis of modern life, *and* the tragic nature of human existence, *and* the inalienable integrity of the human being. The tragic vision, the allegorical meanings of the works, the crafted images, the mythical aspirations, all emphasize the transcending possibilities of man, while the subject matter of the art communicates the agony of now.

These icons of fallen and entrapped humanity are offered as representative of our time. By their dignity, they suggest the possibility that a more advanced mankind will no longer regard these icons as accurate expressions of reality, but only as indicative of that particular era when men could be characterized by the sadness of their lives.

Metaphysical Humanism is the experience it symbolizes, but it is not the experience of crisis that is its subject. The content of the work is a crisis-ridden humanity, but the encompassing form of the work suggests a higher ordering of experience than we can perceive. In Jacob Landau's lithograph, *The Question* (*III. 3*), a response to the holocaust, we see the image of the militarist, the one who compels obedience by force. A group of figures, the victims of force, are splayed against the image of the cross, twisting and falling without control, confused and lost. Yet, we notice that the image of the militarist, the man with the gun, is not terrifying. Nor do the images of his victims shock us with their pain. Instead, these images communicate symbolically the men of force and their victims. The work does not impress us with brutality as an experience; rather, it presents myths that symbolize the brutality of our time. The organization of the surface, the balanced composition, the intricate, swirling linear patterns do not themselves convey acts of violence and disorder, or the life-death struggle. The tension between order and chaos, between man's isolation and his inevitable relatedness, is the symbolic content of the work.

Metaphysical Humanism serves as an art of mediation. It is a timely solace, an art which communicates man's essential worthiness *and* his unworthy situation. Thus, metaphysical Humanism attempts an appraisal of universal modern life. It is concerned with man's fate, his past and his future, but not with the dream and nightmare found in the work of the absurdists.

Metaphysical Humanism does not depict the apocalypse as an event soon upon us. If an artist believes that the demise of the species is imminent, he does not invest the craft and communicate the allegory characteristic of metaphysical Humanist art. Instead, the apocalypse is a metaphor for destiny; a metaphysical insight into a race, capable of so much, and bound, by nature, history, and choice, to wallow in a world many times less fulfilling than that which he can imagine.

The images of metaphysical Humanism are created by emphasizing the figure, and rendering symbolic meaning with gestures. The abstract images, mythical allusions, and nonspecific depiction of social/political events make truth acceptable at a certain level of generality. Its backdrop is the human condition, in which mankind—not a man—is evil. It speaks not of a particular oppression, or of a specific wrong, but becomes concrete only as a way of communicating oppressions and wrongs. The metaphysical Huhumanist views horrific events in the continuum of history. He is able to embrace the greatest number of ambiguities, and aspire to the most cosmic view. Thus, all satisfying metaphysical Humanism has transcendental dimensions.

An understanding of the significance of gesture is the key to discerning the

3. Jacob Landau, *The Question,* from *The Holocaust Suite,* 1968. Lithograph, 15" x 20¼". Courtesy Associated American Artists, New York.

individual styles found within metaphysical Humanism. The images are simplified, and communicate primarily by their interactions, and through the total gestural impact of the work. These mythic images may explode or radiate; they may be compressed or serial; but, in each case, they participate in the central gesture, which is the essential experience. The eye is sent on a journey, which begins with what we see, and later finds itself in the domain of feeling.

Metaphysical Humanism arises out of a combination of the constructional order found in classical art, and the aspirations of German Expressionism: logic and passion, structure and emotion, definition and fantasy, order and irrationality, Blake's marriage of heaven and hell. These opposites are synthesized into one entity.

In all successful metaphysical Humanism, we see tension without ambivalence, opposites without confusion; images indicate our hopeful possibility, and our painful condition. We see mankind subjected to the impact of mankind, while the artist offers the hope that man may once again, someday, be the measure of all things.

Metaphysical Humanism is not an art that compels men to act, to become angry, or to feel a desperate need to change life. It is an art for contemplation. Among the various forms of Humanism, it is the most encompassing perspective of human plight. The work requires a response at a time when it is thought to be in bad taste to ask significant questions of the viewer. Tragedy, which is the genre of this art, is not a "desirable" form of artistic expression.

Those unacquainted with the full range of Humanist expression generally associate Humanism with metaphysical Humanism. Many metaphysical Humanists have been accepted more widely than some of their colleagues. The works of Rico Lebrun, Ben Shahn, Leonard Baskin, Philip Evergood, Jacob Landau, and Mauricio Lasansky have been widely exhibited and universally praised, and it is often their work that has fixed the image of "human concern" and Humanism. Metaphysical Humanism also more often features traditional approaches to the image of the human figure, and consequently is more visually familiar than other forms of Humanist realization, which are often considered too offensive or too risky to receive extensive exposure.

Often, "hotter" Humanists, whose work is riddled with the representation of human suffering, are critical of the detachment of the metaphysical Humanists. They feel that metaphysical Humanism is cool, almost lifeless. But the desperation of the contemporary crisis does not exclude the philosophic message of its more distant drums. Sometimes, the metaphysical Humanist is thought to be afraid of the risk involved in conveying actuality onto the canvas or the plate. Metaphysical Humanists are criticized for making a statement about our time, rather than the experience of it. While this may be true, the implications drawn from it are not. These Humanists consciously make involvement with their work accessible because they do not assault; they will lead the viewer, rather than demand he jump. The tensions in the work, the mythical qualities, and the larger perspective reflect a particular choice, rather than a fear of risk. These Humanists wish to create a more hopeful, a more philosophically satisfying, statement about the potential of life itself. More than other Humanists, they emphasize the strength and nobility of man, even in this time of despair.

The metaphysical Humanists, however,

may take some of the responsibility for the criticism that they exploit content. More than others, they take pains to point out that their work flows directly out of the history of art, and is related to various formal schools and major movements of the twentieth century, such as Abstract Expressionism, Surrealism and German Expressionism. Also, unsuccessful metaphysical Humanism can often be characterized by decorative elements and sentimental statements.

The metaphysical Humanist may, as some believe, pay too many dues to the profession of art; but the dues he pays are only incidental to the perception of crisis he creates. For metaphysical Humanism is, in the end, a dark vision. The metaphysical Humanist knows that, despite unparalleled change, the destructive mechanisms of man are nullified ever so slowly. The metaphysical Humanist might well feel that some of his "hotter" colleagues have not faced up to the ultimate lament, when one forsakes the last vestige of uncritical optimism and understands that, despite the vainglories of human nature itself, the basic drives of the species do not change dramatically. The metaphysical Humanist has a vision of human history that sees life as an endless cycle of aspiration for freedom, and human betrayal.

Perhaps best known for his images of fallen man is Leonard Baskin. Not only has Baskin secured his place in the history of art, but he has also, in the most forceful terms, argued for the kind of Humanistic impulse he represents.

Baskin's work, like that of many other metaphysical Humanists, is aloof from the specific issues of our time. His art is about species man. Using single images without environments, Baskin explodes the existing myths of optimism and progress; he exposes Western man to a re-

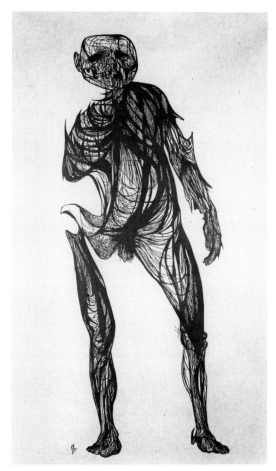

4. Leonard Baskin, *Hydrogen Man,* 1954. Woodcut, 62″ x 31″. Courtesy Kennedy Galleries, Inc., New York.

lentless vivisection. In doing so, Baskin revitalizes many of the myths found within the cultural heritage of two thousand years of Western civilization. His sculptures, such as those of *Icarus, Minotaur,* and *Medusa,* and his graphics, such as *Hydrogen Man* (*III. 4*), *Tormented Man,* and *Hanged Man,* are images of psychological realities—visual icons of human destinies.

As a sculptor and graphic artist, Baskin has developed a distinctive iconography and style. Once his figures are dissected, without flattering paraphernalia, they exist as the exposed nerve endings of humanity. Each of these fleshless figures is concerned with human betrayal, vulnerability, and the outcome of history. Baskin's art removes the delusions men have about themselves. The universality of his work comes from his contention that "the human figure is the image of all men and of one man. It contains all and can express all."[46] His *Everyman,* his *Angel of Death,* his grim armored warriors, his decadent poets laureate, and so forth, are fundamental to Baskin's testimony, and his unique symbolism. His use of anatomy stripped down to fiber, his particular calligraphic line, and the thick black line enclosing rather than disclosing space, identify his style.

While many admire his particular iconography, others are less complimentary to his style. Some feel that style itself mistreats and exploits subject matter. They argue that when Humanistic content is stylized, as it has been in much of Baskin's work, it loses vitality and becomes inauthentic. Furthermore, like Rico Lebrun, the most influential metaphysical Humanist of the century, Baskin has been a major influence on many younger talented Humanist artists; this influence has caused adverse reactions to what many feel is the pervasive Baskin influence in Humanist art. The counter to the charge that Baskin now creates Baskins, that he has influenced too many artists, and that he has not grown sufficiently as an artist, is Baskin's art itself; his popularity has grown enormously, and his work has continued to receive recognition and appreciation. Finally, it must be said that, throughout his career, Baskin has presented us with images of victimized humanity, while formalists explored color, line, and playful form. His forms are not repulsive; they are not designed to anger us. But were it not for decades of Baskin's

art of victims, we might never have come to demand greater force in Humanist art.

Among the many artists initially influenced by Baskin are such gifted artists as Robert Marx, Tom Cornell, Jack Coughlin, Charles Wells, and Sigmund Abeles. These artists have endeavored to create an independent imagery within the metaphysical intention. While some have had difficulty in developing an independent style, they have achieved works of real importance. Critical judgments have harped on their influences. Yet, we must ask with Sigmund Abeles, "Why is it that form without significant/empathetic content is much less embarrassing than content with insignificant form?"[47] The question focuses our attention on the fact that Humanist art is expected to innovate in both content and form. Standards are raised, and inevitably much fine work is rejected unreasonably.

Among the best of the metaphysical Humanists is Jacob Landau, whose achievement arises out of a confident synthesis of major intention and superior craft, accomplished by careful coordination of purpose and technique. As with many metaphysical Humanists, his work is a fusion of multiple visual tensions having allegorical import (*Ill. 5*).

Landau's vehicle for communication through his art is the use of multiple images in single works. The many images in his work are formed into a symbolic unity of great power. Beginning with his suite of *Charades,* Landau has continued to create composite images of people interacting with each other, engaged in frequently meaningless games, acting out in unison a common but unknown destiny. The subject matter emphasizes the search for love, the drama of its transformation into hate or apathy, the pursuit of pleasure for its own sake, and the

5. Jacob Landau, *Holocaust,* from *The Holocaust Suite,* 1968. Lithograph, 15″ x 18½″. Courtesy Associated American Artists, New York.

distorted pleasures of killing, dying, hurting, or destroying. These rituals of human disrelation generally characterize the artist's work.

In *Urbanology Triptych (Colorplate I),* Landau has elevated the charade concept to a global perspective. The *Triptych* is unified by a complex of symbolic masses: The left panel shows a man without arms releasing life from his mouth; a woman in an agony of dance-frenzy; a giant figure with closed eyes, bleeding from the temples with thought-forms rising from his head; all set against a web of industrial structures. We feel the impossibility of communication in the tech-

nological environment. The central panel displays the technological world and the contemporary crisis: astronauts, soldiers, bodies in nets, breathing through tubes, spouting blood, flailing limbs. Smoke and explosions dominate the harsh geometric environment. The right panel shows a massive black, aflame with pain and spirituality, together with other forms either boxed into the urban space or bursting from it, suggesting, perhaps, the emergence of revolutionary awareness and the continuity of violence.

Landau embraces the paradoxical nature of our acts and our possibilities. Hate and love, war and peace, relatedness and alienation, are everywhere found together: a statement of the crisis of our being, and the uncertainty of our future. We see the insistence on order and the acknowledgment of harmony, and, in contrast, the frenzy and disorder of human behavior and social acts. The allegory of the work reveals the artist's belief that out of the struggle against destiny comes the achievement of dignity. This belief is manifest throughout the artist's work. Recently, Landau has enlarged the scope of his work to incorporate a profound engagement with myth: twenty-four foot high stained glass windows of Old Testament prophets, drawings for Dante's *Divine Comedy,* and a suite of woodcuts for the *Revelation of St. John.*

6. Maurice Lasansky, *Nazi Drawing #12,* 1961–66. Pencil, wash, and ink, 72" x 45". Courtesy the artist.

Another artist crucial to the discussion of metaphysical Humanism is Mauricio Lasansky, who is best known for *The Nazi Drawings (Ill. 6).* These life-size drawings are themselves a major contribution to Humanist art. They are among the most powerful allegories of the brutalities of fascism. In his drawings and prints, Lasansky combines terror, isolation, humanity, fear, evil acts, and human possibility with superior craft and a distinctive imagery. Many consider his works to be outstanding achievements within metaphysical Humanism.

The central gesture of Lasansky's *Nazi Drawings* is that of mankind subjected to mankind. The same may be said of metaphysical Humanist Jacob Lawrence, whose work is unique on two accounts: His highly sophisticated iconography, revealing the figure as a role, has given his work a consistent and unique style, and he has dealt with the human dilemma from the specific vision of a black artist. His work is filled with those things that imprison us—wire, masks, lies (*see Ill. 7*). We see the struggle to overcome the prison, a symbol of all that prevents human growth and healthy development. His figures tend to be minimal and highly generalized (*see Ill. 8*). The figures are forms embodying social forces cast in contexts of defeat, anguish, and rebellion. Lawrence's work is a narrative of the struggle of man—first black men, then all men—to cast off the shackles that keep us from fulfilling our potential.

Arnold Belkin turns to the myth of Marat —the champion of freedom—to create a contemporary vision of the death of freedom. In his *Marat* series (*Colorplate II*), he substitutes a computer Marat for David's image of a martyr bleeding; modern man is betrayed and assassinated, not by reactionaries outside him, but by what

7. Jacob Lawrence, *Managerie,* 1964. Gouache, 22″ x 30¾″. Collection Dr. and Mrs. Marvin Sinkoff.

8. Jacob Lawrence, *All Hallow's Eve,* 1960. Tempera, 24″ x 30″. Collection Mr. and Mrs. Walter Nathan.

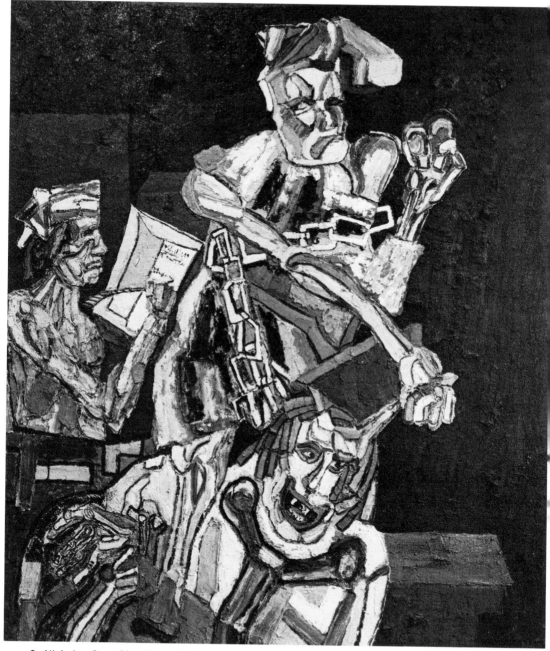

9. Nicholas Sperakis, *Marat Writing His Message to the People,* 1969. Oil, Lucite, and coffee grounds on canvas, 80″ x 50″. Courtesy the artist.

he himself has become. What Marat is destroys Marat. Belkin's use of the airbrush, his multiple images, the hard-edge style, and the architechtonic environment emphasize the depiction of man, once capable of aspiring to what Belkin calls "grandeur," but now stilled by the world. in which he has participated. Nicholas Sperakis, unable to grant man "grandeur" in death, translates the Marat myth into a grotesque comedy (see Ill. 9), a colorful farce of human bondage and betrayal that kills Marat's desire for freedom before Marat is actually assassinated.

Leonard Baskin, Jacob Landau, Jacob Lawrence, and Robert Marx have chosen to make allegorical elements central to their work, and have employed literary devices. Several other metaphysical Humanists use fewer narrative or literary elements, and are still more distant in their overview. While these works have fewer allegorical elements, they create a more cohesive unity between myth and emotional identity.

Best known of these artists is George Segal. While still metaphysical in nature, Segal's work is not specifically involved in allegorical statements. His plaster forms depict myths of human situations. Though the faces of his figures are specifically detailed, the whole of his work constitutes an anonymous mass of humanity, frozen within situational contexts, that evokes response from the viewer. Unconvinced by anger at man's plight, emotionally removed from the apocalypse, Segal chooses to create credible human situations of defeat, alienation, fear, and vacuity.

Segal has been accepted within the aesthetics that predominate. Much has been made of "Segal's unique process of casting people from plaster," a process which "has won him the position of one of the outstanding artistic personalities of the present decade. He has added," continues Phyllis Tuchman, "a new method to the vocabulary of art." Less elaborate is the discussion of his Humanistic intention: "the eloquence of Segal's figures," his "quietly ironic forms with grandeur and nobility," his "darkened, archaeologically literal environments," and his "pathos." More modestly, Segal states, "I want to evoke feeling."[48]

From the criteria that constitute the Humanist aesthetic, and after one takes note of Segal's sculptural innovation, it is necessary to say that his work is uneven. Segal's wish to evoke feeling is not always realized. In some works, the figures are so tentatively expressive, and the situations that comprise the environments of the works sometimes so bland, that Segal's sculptures sometimes become representational art without the Humanist insistence of engagement. When he is successful, as in Girl Learning Against a Doorway, and The Bowery, Segal achieves his Humanist intentions with grace and poetry. Girl Leaning Against a Doorway (Ill. 10) is a powerful work that creates the feeling of anxiety, expectation, and reluctance—the feeling experienced in those moments before the encounter with the world. Outside that door are the unpredictable experiences which will have great impact on another life. The use of the neon as a minimal suggestion of the world effectively conveys the totality of experience. The figure of the girl seems braced and yet reflective, caught in moments of hesitation before . . . before what? Perhaps her expression of anxiety foretells the nature of her next encounter.

The poetic quality of Segal's work is central to appreciation of The Bowery (Ill. 11). Here, the Bowery is not the hu-

10. George Segal, *Girl Leaning Against a Doorway,* 1971. Plaster, wood, plastic, and lights, 108″ x 56″ x 48″. Courtesy Sidney Janis Gallery, New York.

11. George Segal, *The Bowery,* 1970. Plaster, wood, and metal, 96″ x 96″ x 72″. Courtesy Sidney Janis Gallery, New York.

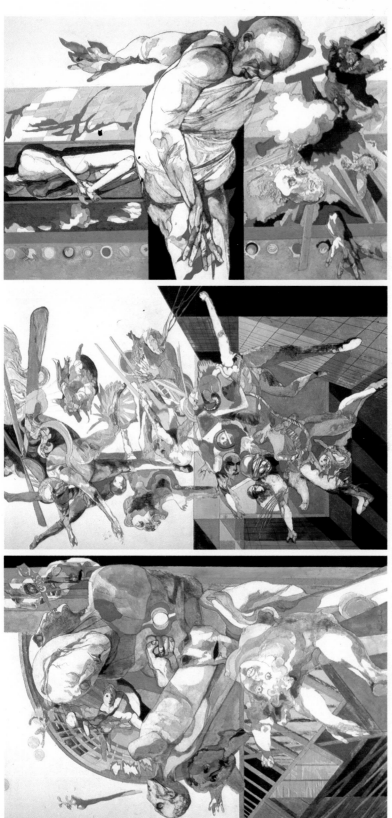

1. Jacob Landau, *Urbanology Triptych*, 1969. Oil on canvas, each panel 48" x 36". Courtesy the artist.

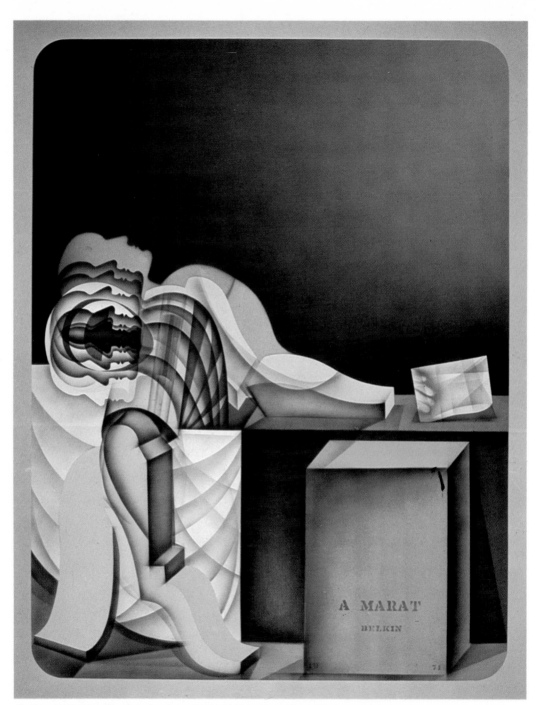

II. Arnold Belkin, *Marat Assassinated I,* 1971. Acrylic, 70" x 55". Courtesy the artist.

III. Duane Hanson, *Derelicts*, 1969. Polyester, fiberglass, mixed media, life-size. Courtesy Neue Gallerie, Aachen, Germany.

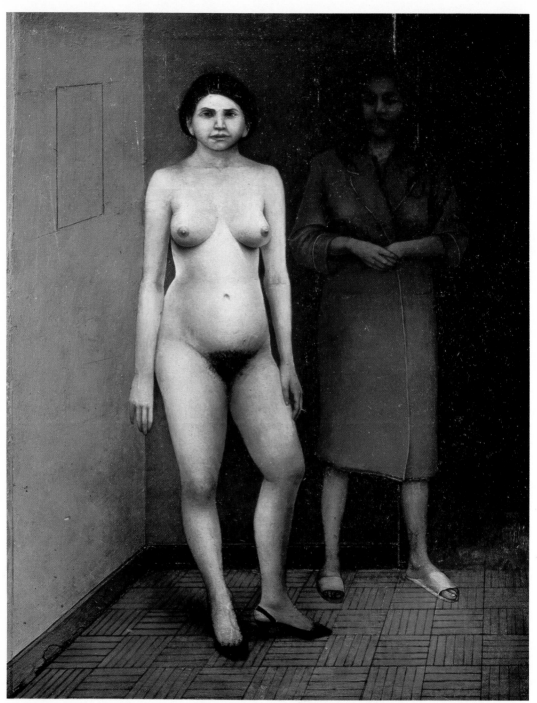

IV. Gregory Gillespie, *Two Women,* 1965. Oil, tempera, synthetic polymer resin, and collage on wood, 14″ x 11″. Collection Whitney Museum of American Art, New York.

man waste, the lost lives, or the actuality we see in Duane Hanson's *Derelicts.* Its feeling is of the insensitivity found in Bowery life. Observing the emaciated drunk on the floor, the standing figure watches with curiosity, with interest, without judgment, the way we watch from our cars and our comfortable homes the suffering of those around us. The Bowery environment is elevated to a metaphysical human situation. In Hanson's *Derelicts (Colorplate III)*, we are not allowed to elevate the situation; we are shoved into the stench of it. Here, we are *in* the Bowery—we are not *seeing* it. In Segal's environment, there is reflection and tension. In Hanson's environment, there is no contemplation, only confrontation. Segal is the metaphysical Humanist whose figures are symbolic; Hanson's images of diminished man offer no retreat. His work is an existential encounter with life. Segal offers a view, and, as a consequence of viewing, we are able to feel. There is a high degree of invitation in the work. Hanson allows no distance; we are not invited to view, but required to witness. Hence, Segal is poetic, essential, and symbolic; the viewer is in another space and time. Hanson makes the viewer a participant; there is no space and time but the present. Segal, the metaphysical Humanist, creates art about life. Hanson, one of the existential Humanists discussed in the next section, creates life through art.

Like Segal, Rudolf Baranik builds a monument to victimized but enduring humanity. In *Napalm Elegy (Ills. 12 and 13)*, a series of his latest works, he employs paint, X rays, and photographs to create a unique approach to collage. It repeats the single image of a burned Vietnamese child, an apt symbol for all the victims Baranik's black mass evokes.

Bombed and beaten, the image admits no defeat. Like twentieth-century man, this image, though in a degraded state, transcends its condition with stature and strength. Baranik's subtle tonality of black and white, his sense of mood, and his individual achievement of tension create the drama of human potential and human actuality. The redundancy of the image, and its inherent strength, even when presented as an X ray, inspire in the viewer admiration of the vitality of what is normally regarded as merely a record of one of the century's victims. Though discussions of the artist's work have tended to dwell on how similar Baranik's dark mood is to the black paintings of Ad Reinhardt, the outstanding feature of his art is not its compatibility with the new abstraction, but its relentless commitment to the expression of feeling about a chosen content.

Balcomb Greene, once an articulate spokesman for abstraction in art, has in recent years, turned to a poetic form of metaphysical Humanism. Greene's images are of a monumental humanity eroded by time and progress—by history *(see Ill. 14)*. The powerful image is accentuated by its placement within ruins or ruin-like structures. We can feel a once-great being now in a fallen state. The experience is of the dissolution of the species, here created through the use of paint and light to erode and dissolve the figure and its environment. Like Shelley's Ozymandias, Greene's figures ask that we "look upon my works, ye mighty, and despair." Again, like many of the metaphysical Humanists, Greene's works do not scream out, "Look what we are doing to ourselves." In more somber, quieter, less passionate terms, it says, "Look what has become of us." And, unlike the images of diminished man that soon follow,

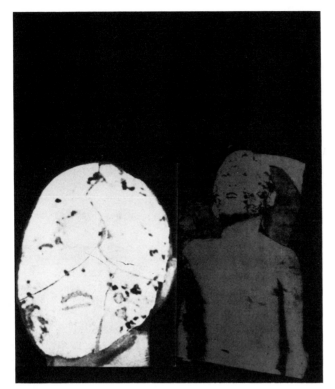

12. Rudolf Baranik, *Napalm Elegy,* Series #3, 1970. Collage of photostat, X-ray, and acrylic on canvas, 38″ x 26″. Courtesy the artist.

13. Rudolf Baranik, *Napalm Elegy,* Series #12, 1970. Collage of photostat, X-ray, and acrylic on canvas, 62″ x 72″. Courtesy the artist.

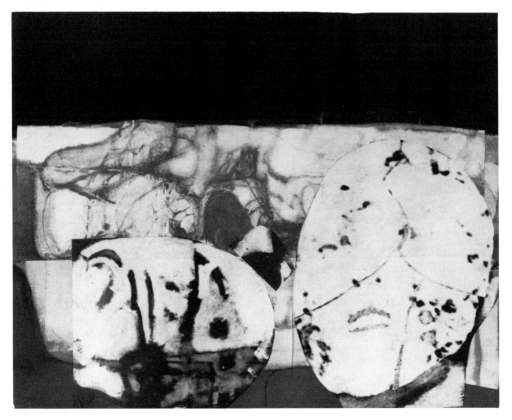

14. Balcomb Greene, *The Steps,* 1971. Oil on canvas, 66″ x 53″. Courtesy the artist.

15. Antonio Lopez-Garcia, *El Water,* 1966. Oil on board, approx. 79″ x 39½″. Collection Mr. and Mrs. Enrico Donati, New York.

Greene's images suffer erosion without the loss of beauty. As in the work of Baskin, Landau, Segal, and Baranik, Greene strongly points to the possibility of fulfillment beyond our time.

Another artist who achieves a similar communication is Spanish painter and sculptor Antonio Lopez-Garcia. His canvases, like Baranik's, are filled with a somber atmosphere, a cheerless and uncompromising gray environment. His pictures are dark and violent, with a bleakness that characterizes his perception of the environment. And, like Baranik, Lopez-Garcia has infused painting with sculptural elements to create a stark, moving image of great intensity. In *El Water (Ill. 15)* he has created a work of intimacy, a private glimpse into human reality that is filled with metaphysical and symbolic implications; no longer a toilet, this room

16. Antonio Lopez-Garcia, *Los Novios,* 1964. Relief on polychromed wood, approx. 33½″ x 33½″ x 4″. Courtesy Emily D.
Staempfli, New York.

17. Antonio Lopez-Garcia, *Mujer Dormida,* 1960–64. Relief on
polychromed wood, approx. 47″ x 79″ x 8″. Courtesy Gallery
Galatea, Torino.

18. Gaston Orellana, *Crucifixion* (triptych), 1971. Oil on canvas, approx. 21'11" x 8'2". Courtesy the artist.

with its machines and gadgets, like the shield of Achilles, tells the history of the race. Here is the sad and sanitary universe that we all experience, alone. Many of the metaphysical Humanists create tension by what Tennessee Williams once called "snatching the eternal out of the desperately fleeting." The transitory event, the private time, the moments of emotion before the intrusion of the world, are felt through this work. *Los Novios* (*Ill. 16*) and *Mujer Dormida* (*Ill. 17*) are typical of Lopez-Garcia's created frozen moments—a suspended moment of farewell, fllled with the sense of contemporaneity. One anticipates, seconds later, an event which will occur to collapse the reality fixed before our eyes.

Baranik, Segal, and Lopez-Garcia attempt to induce, rather than provoke or demand, responses. The works have mysterious qualities, through which the viewer is compelled to determine relationships. Other metaphysical Humanists are more direct in their imagery. Gaston Orellana fills his large, colorful canvases with the heap of humanity, placed in its

death postures by the acts of men. His *Crucifixion* (*Ill. 18*) incorporates an uncompromising judgment of contemporary history. "It is the aim of my work," says Orellana, "to be the mirror where desolation and disconsolation blow and fall: life without death; premature deaths; persecutions and judgments."[49]

Orellana has created a distinctive iconography and painting style (*see Ill. 19*). His figures are the bag of the body, collapsed and without vitality, placed in the positions of their devitalization. Orellana's use of subtle color gives his paintings an organic but deathlike atmosphere, almost as though a wind of death or violence had swept up an otherwise fertile and promising human situation. After the wind has passed, we find the remains of what was once a cohesive and functioning species. Though Orellana's work is in no way visually similar to the paintings of Leon Golub, which are presented later in the book, both metaphysical Humanists have very similar conceptualizations of the Humanist intention.

Malformed humanity is the imagery in

19. Gaston Orellana, *Toque de queda,* 1970. Oil on canvas, approx.
10′6″ x 13′1″. Courtesy the artist.

20. Manuel Ayaso, *Pleamar,* 1968. Goldpoint, watercolor, and gesso
on paper, 9⁹⁄₁₆″ x 8⅞″. Collection Mr. and Mrs. Nick B. Williams,
California.

21. Manuel Ayaso, *Artist's Reflections,* 1963. Pastel, wash, pen, and ink. 40″ x 45″. Collection Dr. and Mrs. S. Lifschutz, New Jersey.

22. Nicholas Sperakis, *Bowery Love Make,* 1968. Oil, Lucite, and coffee grounds on canvas, 50″ x 80″. Courtesy the artist.

the work of Manuel Ayaso. Ayaso's silver-point and goldpoint drawings with water-color washes combine a Surrealistic fantasy with an intention of metaphysical Humanism (*see Ill. 20*). Dwarfed, suspicious, confused, ugly humanity peers back from the world, as if to call attention to the essential nature of what it is we have become. Ayaso's vision is personal, bleak, and without relief. Filled with faces and figures which we might find repulsive and, at the same time, uncomfortably familiar, his work is the recognition of an inner world that is confused and nightmarish (*see Ill. 21*). Ayaso's comment on his own work is revealing: "Look at the creased, weather-beaten and starved faces, the hollow pockets and glassy eyes of the peasants and poor people from where I come, and you see why I paint the way I do."[50]

Nicholas Sperakis, a painter and print-maker, is a member of a group of talented and articulate Humanists who call themselves the Rhino Horn. Sperakis's art reveals the spectacle of the human circus, but this circus does not make you laugh (*see Ill. 22*); it is a dehumanized dungeon into which are placed human figures resembling outworn machines, dummies, and farcical robotic clowns devoid of those qualities we perceive as human. Sperakis's imagery is of a defiled and ridiculous humanity, vulgar creatures of modern life. Symbolic man is torn, broken, and of no further use.

Peter Passuntino, another metaphysical Humanist in the Rhino Horn group, creates a strong imagery of vivisection and natural forms. Passuntino reduces men to the organic, to earth, vegetation, veins, arteries and inanimate forms. Here,

23. Peter Passuntino, *Who Are You? What Is Your Name?*, 1970. Oil on canvas, 66½" x 90". Courtesy the artist.

24. Jonah Kinigstein, *The Nazi Butchers,*
1970. Oil on Masonite, 6' x 4'. Courtesy the artist.

the conqueror of Nature is conquered by human nature, and man returns once again into the stuff of the world. If Bosch saw the Garden of Delights as a vision of human sin, Passuntino sees only a garden in which man's actions have brought him back to decay, and to the life cycle of death and diffusion as in *Who are you? What is your name?* (*Ill. 23*).

Jonah Kinigstein creates the circus of history. Casting contemporary institutions in their historical robes, Kinigstein views the human past as an ever-renewing history of betrayal, greed, and alienation. Against what he considers the Madison Avenue approach to art, Kinigstein's canvases are allegorical graveyards for the corrupt and the powerful.

As we see in *The Nazi Butchers* (*Ill. 24*), his images of degeneracy are taken from the clergy, the political establishment, and the history of betrayers.

All these works, from the collapsed bags of figures in the work of Orellana to the poetic forms of Segal and Lopez-Garcia, to the monumental strength of Baranik's image of the Vietnamese, demonstrate the nature of metaphysical Humanism, which is, as Arnold Belkin put it, "concerned with man, his mental landscape, his inner structure, his vision, his dehumanization and with the affirmation of his persona"[51] (*see Ill. 25*).

The various forms of Humanist art derive their individuality by the way in which the artist creates both man's de-

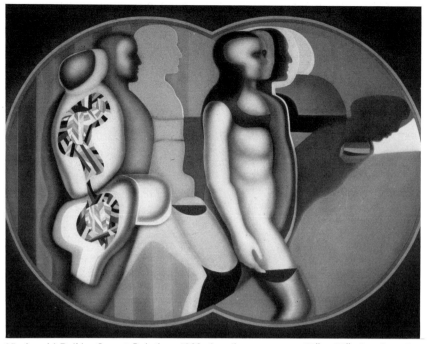

25. Arnold Belkin, *Secret Painting,* 1969. Acrylic on canvas, 62" x 80". Courtesy the artist.

humanization *and* "the affirmation of his persona." Among the metaphysical Humanists are found some artists who emphasize poetic elements to the degree that their art is primarily a lyrical statement. While there are many artists working in this direction, so many of them create an unconvincing romanticism that there are relatively few satisfying works. Most lyrical Humanists create man out of context. Perhaps believing that idealization will be a better model for changed behavior, these artists often create a vision of human beings freed of the technological society, free of pathologies now prevalent. Unfortunately, only rarely do we find lyrical Humanism that is credible, that can speak with a believable optimism, that is affirmative within the context of our world —not outside of it. Lyrical Humanism achieves its optimism by virtue of its distance. But this distance is sometimes so great that the work created is no longer

contemporary, and reverts to a time before the twentieth century had defined itself and made such works obviously sentimental.

An exception to the general trend is the art of Romare Bearden, who is most known for his honest and dignified investigation of the black experience. His collages of paper and synthetic polymer painting on composition board identify his technique. Bearden's work constitutes a portraiture of black experience and individual black lives within the environments of our time. Because there is no private space in the tenement life Bearden depicts, he chooses to create works that overflow with multiple images. Throughout his art is the vibratory feeling of interaction, multiple experience, and simultaneous events. He compresses time, and manages to convey the dread and *élan* of street life.

Bearden builds his collages from bits

26. Romare Bearden, *The Dove,* 1964. Collage of paper and synthetic polymer paint on composition board, 13⅜″ x 18⅞″. Collection The Museum of Modern Art, New York.

27. Romare Bearden, *Black Manhattan,* 1969. Collage of paper and synthetic polymer paint on composition board, 25⅜″ x 21″. Collection Mr. and Mrs. Theodore W. Kheel, New York.

28. Lester Johnson, *Emerging Crowd,*
1970. Oil on canvas, 68" x 60".
Courtesy Martha Jackson Gallery,
New York.

and pieces of found images. He incorporates a sense of randomness, and the
arbitrary aspects of black life. In *The
Dove* (*Ill. 26*), the white bird of peace sur-
vives the tumultuous life that exists within
partitioned stone and brick structures.
Human beings spill out of the houses,
and cluster on the streets in front of us.
They are vital, alive, but densely populated. In *Black Manhattan* (*Ill. 27*), Bearden creates the feeling of humans confined by space and time. The faces in the
windows watch the action below. The
work is filled with fire escapes, apart-
ment dwellings, street watchings; it is
filled with waiting, with black time. Here
is the dual perception of the conditions
of multiple family housing, and the dignity and strength of the human figures
within, compressed into a metaphysical
statement about life in our time.

Bearden's affirmation—an affirmation

created in the context of contemporary
experience—derives its strength from his
belief that the life-style of the black in
America is "perhaps the richest because
it is the one life style that is talking about
life and about the continuation of life . . .
and through all of the anguish—the joy
of life."[52]

Lester Johnson's art can be related to
this context. Johnson creates paintings
that cannot contain the many figures entrapped within their frames (*see Ill. 28*).
Once the practitioner of abstract painting, Johnson now depicts the crush and
overcrowded lives of the bourgeois.
Jammed together, bumping and pushing
one another, lost in a multiple sameness,
Johnson's identically clad, bowler-hatted,
carbon-copy men accept their sardine
existence without rebellion. Yet, each
individual figure possesses enormous
strength and dignity. Constrained by his

condition, each one is dignified by his possibility. As Johnson put it, he wants "to prove that man is more than a man—to put him on a pedestal. The human and the monumental are contradictory, but I wanted to put them together."[53]

Bearden and Johnson are exceptions. Painters who strive for a lyrical Humanism are rarely as successful as the lyrical sculptors, probably because the three-dimensional image itself, capable of creating greater presence and volume, is inherently more convincing. Elbert Weinberg is among the best sculptors working in this direction. In *Charon #1* (*Ill. 29*), we see a sculptural image of the figure we are told took man across the river to hell.

The artists discussed in this chapter have avoided art that is saccharine or sentimental. Working out of a vision that is uniquely their own, they have created an art that incorporates today's crisis within a perspective that transcends it. The artists represented in the following section are unable to provide relief, hope, and possibility. The world is all. Perhaps, with Sartre, they might agree that "hell is other people."

Existential Humanism: Images of Diminished Man

The existential Humanists maintain no emotional distance from the experiences they create. The existential Humanist is "hot." His images of diminished man are confrontational. The artist wants to provoke intense emotions. While the art tells less than the allegorical works we have seen in the previous section, images of diminished man *are the experience* the metaphysical Humanists *symbolize.*

The existential Humanists insist that the viewer recognize and respond to their

29. Elbert Weinberg, *Charon #1,* 1964. Bronze, 6' high. Courtesy the artist.

defiled images. One may look at meta-physical Humanism and ask, "Is it true that life is like this?" When dealing with existential Humanism, the viewer is compelled to ask, "How did this come to be?" Existential Humanism is the collective nightmare, the revelation of the crimes of the twentieth century.

The images of diminished man are visual metaphors, re-creating the painful experience of the individual man in the technological era. They are formally interesting, partly because each artist must create his own iconography, as well as a fresh rendering of the figure within a collective expression of pained and anguished images. However their specific techniques vary, all the artists here recognize that, among all the vehicles for human expression, there exist few avenues for the public communication of pain and anger, beyond visual art. The visual image created by the individual artist is one primary embodiment of the sensibility of the disenfranchised.

The existential Humanist journeys into the eye of the hurricane, the maelstrom of our century. His is a release of anger, repulsion, and despair at an impotent, fragmented, partial humanity. Against the celebration of progress and products, civilization and futuristic optimism, these images bring us back to the price some have had to pay for the "advance" of "modern" man.

A quality common to most of these images is the distortion of the figure. In contrast to the strong allegorical elements of metaphysical Humanism, those distorted images of diminished man are created to provoke strong emotions. The communication of subject matter, and the form through which the communication occurs, are one.

Critics often claim that many of the existential Humanists are obsessively preoccupied with the grotesque. Existential Humanism is sometimes characterized as "monster" art. In fact, existential Humanism will be successful only insofar as the artist creates disturbing, not grotesque, images. The disturbing image wants to affect the viewer, wants to tell him something about himself, and the world he lives in. A disturbing image will not let you off the hook, will not let you believe that the image you see is outside of your experience. The grotesque in art quickly reduces to novelty, to a fascinating oddity: at first shocking, because of its curious nature, but, after a time, easily dismissable as eccentric expression. Truly disturbing images cannot be dismissed; they remain in the visual memory, continually stimulating it with the accuracy of their communication.

Existential Humanist images are disturbing because they ask that reality be changed, that victims no longer characterize the species, that we do something to make this mutilated, ugly humanity passé, no longer an accurate representation of human lives. They are counter-cultural images, which announce to society that, as long as brutality and inhumanity arre the results of social behavior, the artist will continue to resurrect the dead and maimed as appropriate contributions to our cultural life.

Unfortunately, many critics and art historians think that, if a work of art makes us feel bad, it is a bad work. Though most critics are more sophisticated in their approach, the result is the same whenever these works are dismissed *because* the artist achieved his intention—disturbing the viewer. The rationale for his arbitrary dismissal is often based on the position that, because artists in the past have effectively communicated human suffering, there is nothing new in this work. Rarely do we hear, however, of another art rejected because it is too joyous, or because joy has been successfully communicated in the art of the past. Others say that the world is already too dismal, that they have no wish to see the world in their art. They turn to art, they say, for enrichment, and freedom from the social/political milieu. The wish to identify good art with effective escape mechanisms is itself confirmation of the alienation this art communicates.

The images of diminished man constitute a macabre house of horrors, populated by outcomes of history. Each is an exhibition of man's possibilities, ridiculed and tortured by man's actions. The paintings and prints scream their anguish, as we bear witness to what noble images are defiled, not by the artist, but by the actions of society. Their most profound communication like that of Mother Courage, comes as a scream that cannot be heard. This is the fun house of broken promises, of denied aspirations, of corrupted possibilities. If the metaphysical Humanist awakens in us the feeling of solace, the existential Humanist creates the experience of solace in chains. The images of diminished man call us out of our indifference, and ask us to be angered by what we have allowed ourselves to become.

The works of diminished man offer less invitation than other realizations of the Humanist intention. They repel or haunt us, but never allow distance. In contrast to the fusion of art and man characteristic of metaphysical Humanism, these images of diminished man represent the fusion of art and life. In their most mythical aspect, these victims of the environment symbolize the expulsion from the technological Eden; in their most concrete form, they are the victims of the systems we use to mutilate each other.

The betrayal of human potential, and the anguish of diminished man, are the themes of existential Humanist Nancy

30. Nancy Grossman, *Three Heads,* 1971. Patent leather and zippers over wood and polyester resin, each 16¾" high. Courtesy the artist.

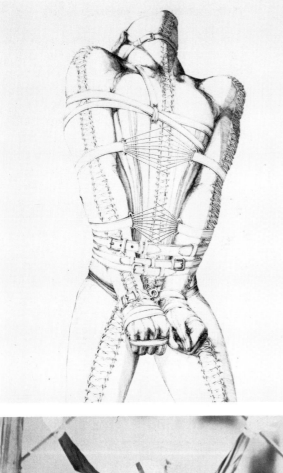

31. Nancy Grossman, *Male Figure,* 1970. Ink on paper, 45½″ x 34½″. Courtesy Cordier & Ekstrom Gallery, New York.

32. Larry Johnson, *Bondage #7,* 1971. Photo process on aluminum, 25½″ x 21½″. Courtesy the artist.

Grossman. Her sculptured heads (*see Ill. 30*) are formed by stitches growing across faces. Each head is encapsulated, enmeshed, confined by the material. The head is choked by the mask. The leather is stretched tight across the flesh. Frozen in the face of pain, entrapment, and enslavement, with zippers and snaps, the heads struggle to open themselves, to give out the scream, the "primal scream" of anguished response to the brutality of our time.

The tension in her work is overwhelming. But the voice cannot utter sound; the tongue is held by the pressure of the casing. The world is the prison of man. How foolish seem the critics who impassionately discuss the use of leather as a new material for art, or those who attribute this work to an obsession with sado-masochistic fantasy. The work wants no response except a physical sensation of claustrophobia, a dizziness, a feeling that it is my head, my tongue, my prison.

Grossman's two-dimensional images work differently. They are less "things," and more allegorical icons. In *Male Figure (Ill. 31)*, Grossman creates the experience of the bound body. Unlike Michelangelo's slaves and prisoners, embedded in rock, and yet given the potential for freedom, Grossman creates an inescapable bondage, maintained by the assassins of Marat, who are always willing to replace a broken strap.

Larry Johnson is another artist who focuses on the theme of the bound man (*see Ill. 32*). He uses society's images from books, newspapers, and magazines, in a novel photographic process, creating impressions on aluminum plates. Johnson converts images designed to intrigue the curious into isolated metaphors of contemporary captivity.

The works of Grossman and Johnson are expressions of confinement and struggle. The paintings of Tony Canger are expressions of confinement and apathy. Canger's art is filled with a scream, but his selfless images are incapable of its utterance. The couples in Canger's work have no relationship to each other (*see Ill. 33*). The nuclear family has been atomized. Locked in their roles, surrounded by the plastic technology of their home, they exist oblivious to the perimeter of life, symbolized by images of nature, which they cannot see. In their private world, their earned environment, they live the mechanical death, filled with the illusion that they have avoided vacuity. They sleep in life, and the bed upon which they are stilled is composed of the possessions that we are forever reminded are intended to provide happiness. In *Birth (Ill. 34)*, Canger creates an archetypal image of woman reduced to breeder. She gives birth, in a ritual of denial, to new life. A metaphor of damnation, this child is excrement for the future.

While Canger's figures are bound by inner constraints of unconscious apathy, Gregory Gillespie's images are bound by alienated defiance. His figures resist and oppose human connection. There is absolutely no invitation into Gillespie's paintings. His figures are outside of us, unapproachable, from another time and place (*see Ill. 35*). It is impossible for the viewer to project optimism, caring, spring, vitality, warmth, or feeling onto the icy cold texture of the canvas. The eye is sent back to the brain. No longer able to believe, to love, to permit enthusiasm, these are images of finished human beings.

Nothing happens in a Gillespie painting. There is action without purpose, function without the illusion of importance. The images exist without meaning,

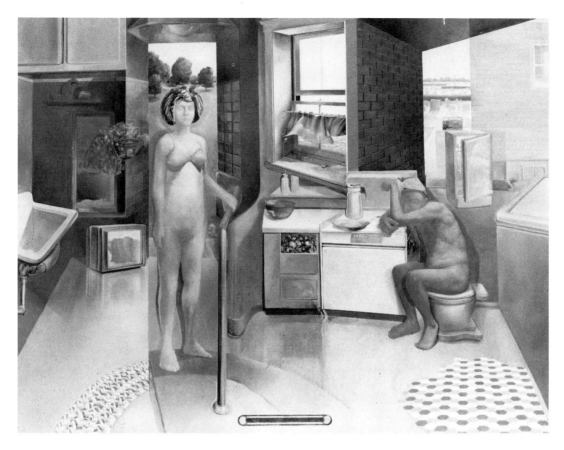

33. Tony Canger, *Family,* 1968. Oil on canvas, 6′ x 8′. Courtesy the artist.

34. Tony Canger, *Birth,* 1966. Oil on canvas, 5′ x 4′. Courtesy the artist.

35. Gregory Gillespie, Untitled portrait, 1967. Mixed media, 15½″ x 11½″. Collection Joseph H. Hirshhorn Foundation, New York.

36. Gregory Gillespie, *Woman with Baby (Crying)*, 1968. Oil and tempera on wood, 14″ x 11″. Collection I. Schwartz, New York.

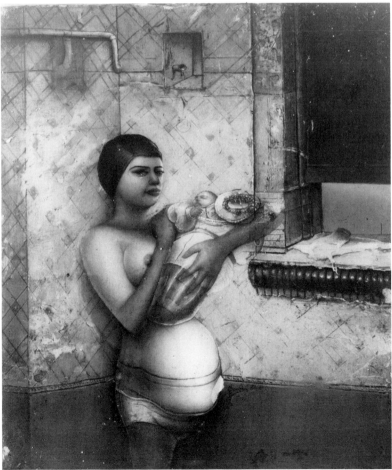

surrounded by decay. In *Woman with Baby (Crying)* (*III. 36*), the mother knows she is being watched; and she, in turn, watches back. But she will not allow contact or communication; her eyes are filled with an impassionate hatred. She knows you have nothing to offer her. In *Two Women* (*Colorplate IV*), the figures are separate, yet related. The young girl is the clay from which the old bronze is fashioned. The younger woman has the potential for sensuality, for sexuality; she seems open to the experience of life, of bodies, of pleasure. But the expression on the face of the old woman, perhaps her mother, perhaps her madam, is confident and cynical. From the shadows, she watches, knowing that this potential cannot be fulfilled. The young girl is

37. George Tooker, *The Tellers,* 1968. Egg tempera on gesso panel, 23¼″ x 15½″. Courtesy Frank Rehn Gallery, New York.

38. George Tooker, *The Ward,* 1970. Egg tempera on gesso panel, 20″ x 30″. Collection Mr. and Mrs. Joel Wm. Harnett, New York.

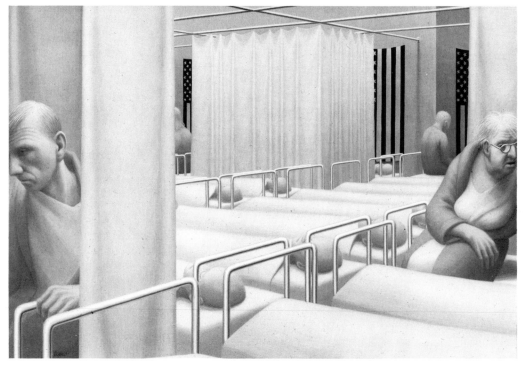

caught in a process whose ends are known. Here are their lives, their stories, their hopes, and their despair. They are untouchable, and ultimately unknowable. Yet, Gillespie's paintings are so arresting, so demanding, we cannot avoid them, or pass them by, or give them little notice; we cannot escape their anxiety, their loneliness, their sorrow, their solitude, and their weariness.

The figures of George Tooker are bound in a conspiracy of silence. The icy texture found in Gillespie's work is transformed into an all-pervading atmosphere in Tooker's paintings. Here, in Tooker's art, we have the successful integration of man and his created system. The hospital, the supermarket, the bank, are the same environment, requiring the same mentality (see Ill. 37). The figures are collected in a communal hopelessness, a universal agreement that there will be no opposition. Silently, they perform their ritualized dehumanized roles. Tooker sees reduced life as reportage. In his work, there is nothing beyond the facts of existence; the blind unfeeling environment of institutional and corporate life. He has turned the technological environment back on itself. The system runs smoothly, the human beings are efficient. But there are no values other than function, no emotions involved in the completion of tasks. Life is the routine from which Tooker's figures never awaken. The viewer is allowed no illusions; he must deal with experience as it appears in the system he serves. In The Ward (Ill. 38), the American flag, symbol of a country which claims to be humane, is ironically placed in the room of America's aged; they are left alone and forgotten, waiting for death.

If Tooker's figures are bound by silence, the half-formed amorphic images created by Hiram Williams are bound by flesh. Fragmented and partial, they are replica humans. The palpable flesh is skin stretched across cardboard skeletons; these people have no bones, no structure, no cartilage (see Ill. 39). In the bag of putty flesh are stuck eyes; they stare emotionlessly, without recognition. The parading women are practically faceless, consisting only of flesh, breasts, stomachs, and limbs (see Ill. 40). Without spirit and mind, they exist as disjointed bodies, façades of purposeless human beings. In Chorus Line with Hose (Ill. 41), Williams turns to a collage approach that more graphically emphasizes flat, mindless figures, hung on existence rather than involved in it. Like scarecrows to keep away the living, they hang limp and lifeless.

Mindlessness, obedience to the authoritarian ethic, and the loss of self are frequent themes in Humanist art. The single image of Robert Marx's Fishhook Man (Ill. 42), and the multiple images of Seymour Rosofsky's Unemployment Agency (Ill. 43), create experiences of the ways human beings have traded their sensitivity and determination for smoother adjustment to the requirements of the technological environment. Here are human beings who have taken "the easy way out," "avoided trouble," chosen to be "inconspicuous," and who, by refusing to oppose the forces that dehumanize them, have become fixtures in the sterile environments that now contain them.

Michael Fauerbach creates a summary visual metaphor for life-in-death (see Ill. 44). "The subject of my work," he states, "is a life style that gets worse as it gets 'better'; an environment that becomes inhuman at the same time that it becomes increasingly 'man-made.' "[54] Fauerbach completes the ritual of bondage by imprisoning man by death and defeat. This communication is achieved by the repeated image of man dying at the steps of the monolith. Here, the creation of man sits prepared for eternity—cold, gray, steel, asphalt, cement, and iron. Man created *that,* but he could not find a way to live.

The visual image of death in the technological environment is perhaps best known through the work of Ernest Trova. Trova has created the marriage of technological form and human body (*see III. 45*). Man is not found dead at the steps of the monolith; man *is* the monolith. Trova's figures of mechanized man serve as forecasts of the twenty-first century. Man is stripped down to metal; shiny, chromed, alloyed. Fallen man is machine-man; the human being is the tooled functionary.

39. Hiram Williams, *Group of Gazers,* 1964. Acrylic and oil on canvas, 50″ x 50″. Courtesy Lee Nordness Galleries, New York.

40. Hiram Williams, *Three Women*, 1959. Oil on canvas, 96" x 72". Courtesy the artist.

41. Hiram Williams, *Chorus Line with Hose*, 1970. Acrylic with mixed media and collaged nylon hoses, 8'2" x 10'. Courtesy Lee Nordness Galleries, New York.

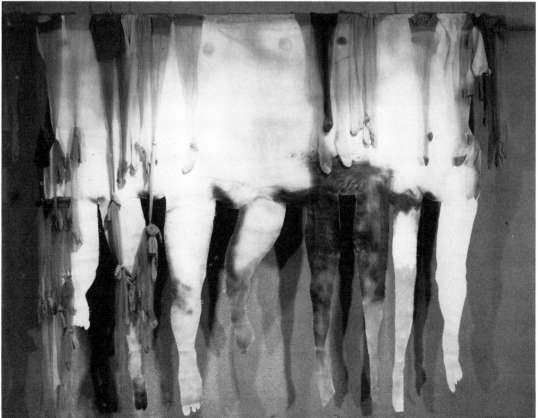

42. Robert Marx. *Fishhook Man,* from *Crime Trial Portfolio,* 1970. Colored etching, 4¾″ x 4½″. Courtesy the artist.

43. Seymour Rosofsky, *Unemployment Agency,* 1958. Oil on canvas, 51¾″ X 67¾″. Courtesy the artist.

44. Michael Fauerbach, *Suicide,* 1969. Oil on canvas and Masonite,
69″ x 49″ x 30½″. Courtesy the artist.

45. Ernest Trova, *Study #53* (*Hoop Man*), 1968. Nickel-plated bronze,
13″ x 10″. Courtesy The Pace Gallery, New York.

46. Alan Bermowitz, *Sunday Trench,* 1966. Pen and ink, 16″ x 14″. Collection Mel Auston, New York.

Some images of diminished man are passive; the vitality of human beings forever destroyed. Other images reach out to us, want us to experience their brutality. They are images of overt confrontation. They insist we see them. The passive images no longer possess the energy to communicate their despair. They do not assault us; they do not frighten us. From a distance, we can empathize with their sorrow. Sometimes an artist will create both passive and active images—Francis Bacon, for example; sometimes an artist concentrates on one or the other. However artists may differ in their methods, the outcome is the same: We are implicated in the destruction we see.

The drawings of Alan Bermowitz are an active accusation of our participation in, and toleration of, another's torture. Bermowitz throws at us bodies mutilated by wars, and minds mutilated by obedience and insensitivity to destructive values (*see III. 46*). Crippled, blinded, and brutalized, these figures are seen to participate in their own torture.

At first, it seems Bermowitz has assumed a satirical stance, but the figures themselves, and the somber atmosphere of the works, transcend irony, and depict a powerfully drawn experience of human abuse. Transformed into human garbage, these figures of diminished man tell us that, if we do not wish to see decimated human beings, we have to change the world that creates them. In *"Gee Whiz, the Army Sure Knows How to Take Care of Us Guys"* (*III. 47*), Bermowitz creates

47. Alan Bermowitz, *"Gee Whiz, The Army Sure Knows How to Take Care of Us Guys,"* 1967. Pen and ink, 14" x 16". Collection Mel Auston, New York.

an environment of images conveying the inhumanity of war, and the degradation of man that results from it. It is impossible to erect slogans, evoke patriotism, cold war ideology, and obtuse theories of freedom and dominoes. Here, woman is turned into a carnal beast, a body with a hole, with whom the maimed and wounded soldiers take pleasure in a bestial mockery of the sexual act. The atmosphere of stench, decay, and rotting flesh is achieved by Bermowitz's baroque quality, his exaggerated imagery, his reptilian humans—an iconography that is absorbed within the powerful experience of the work. Most patrons would not like to live with this work, but why is it that they are willing to live with war?

48. Renzo Vespignani, *Mascherata—come Lautrec,* 1971. Oil and graphite on canvas, approx. 76" x 44". Courtesy Galeria Il Fante di Spade, Rome.

49. Peter Milton, *Return,* 1969. Etching and engraving, 12" x 18". Courtesy the artist.

The Humanist knows that no century has universalized warfare to the degree ours has; no century has been as much affected by war, and none has seen so many killed. The art of Vespignani is a heresy to the doctrine of war. His deformed figures are placed against slogan-stained walls etched by bullets and blood (*see Ill. 48*). Man is turned into beast; his mind is driven into its inner recesses. Unable to comprehend what has been done to him, he has reverted to another form of life better directed by natural instinct and the random selection of the species than by the often eulogized qualities of civilization.

Peter Milton, with Wordsworth, believes that the child is father of the man. The uniformed soldier in *Return* (*Ill. 49*) is respected, though he is an instrument of destruction. But the mad child we find repulsive. How strange, is it not, that we find madness in children more appalling than madness in adults.

The etchings of J. L. Steg are of the collected victims of war (*see Ills. 50 and 51*). Steg has isolated an individual's fatal torment. The figures are token; they symbolize the pain of the millions by the agony of the one.

Arthur Secunda and Reiner Schwarz, both printmakers, present the two faces of man in war. Schwarz's *Der Stechelm* (*Ill. 52*) is the blind face of battle. The helmeted figure is revealed to us only by the open bestial mouth, the set teeth, and the hidden personality. He is the force which compels destruction. Secunda takes off the helmet (*see Ill. 53*), dissects the head, and finds a mind of nuts and bolts, an image of mechanical brain and clockwork cerebrum. These works communicate the violence that results from the actions of a conditioned, programmed, unaware mechanical humanity.

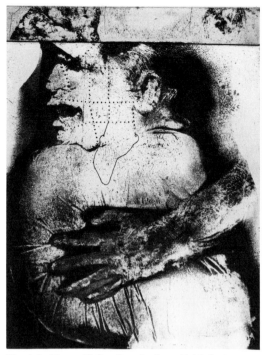

50. J. L. Steg, *#3 Conformity,* from 7 *Attributes Suite,* 1970. Etching, 24″ x 18¼″. Courtesy the artist.

51. J. L. Steg, *Ecce Homo!,* 1970. Etching, 29⅓″ x 24″. Courtesy the artist.

Perhaps the most disturbing art on the theme of war by a contemporary Humanist is created by the Israeli Yehuda Ben-Yehuda. His work symbolizes the agony of millions by the pain of many (*see Ill. 54*). He re-creates the mass grave, the burial pit of the century. Here lie the bodies of the multitudes who were sacrificed in the name of "progress" and false ideals. These twisted, contorted figures constitute a portraiture of those who have been robbed of their lives. This holocaust tells us what we have been capable of doing to each other. No one would like to see this work, and that is why it must be seen.

Yehuda Ben-Yehuda creates his art in a way that is analogous to the historical process that created the victims the art represents. He starts with fully alive, healthy bodies, in order to fashion the agonized mass of figures that comprise the environment he creates. In the photo-graph of Ben-Yehuda's studio (*Ill. 55*), the artist is seen applying the first coat of plaster to the sensuous body of his model. From such bodies are made the heap of humanity that rests on the floor. Why is it, the work asks, that we find offensive in art that which we have rationalized as inevitable in life?

Specific offenses to humanity are the subjects of Edward Kienholz. In his *The State Hospital* (*Ill. 56*), bondage, defeat, and disease are incorporated into one environmental sculpture. The visual degradation of these images is further heightened by the use of the smells of waste and decay as part of the environment. Kineholz attacks the value structures of society by showing society its own prisoners of life. These figures have been sentenced to an early death as a medieval punishment for their crime of sickness.

Kienholz's *The Wait* (*Ill. 57*) is another

52. Reiner Schwarz, *Der Stechelm,* 1969. Lithograph, 11¾" x 8¼". Courtesy Associated American Artists, New York.

53. Arthur Secunda, *The Anarchist,* 1967. Serigraph, 23" x 16⅞". Courtesy Associated American Artists, New York.

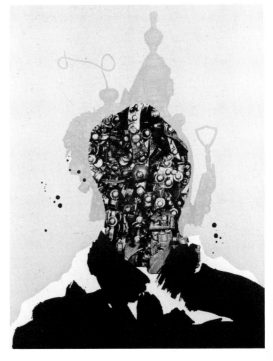

54. Yeduha Ben-Yehuda, *Mass of Figures* (detail),
    1967. Latex and foam, life-size. Courtesy the
    artist.

55. Yehuda Ben-Yehuda, photograph of the artist at
    work, 1967. Courtesy the artist.

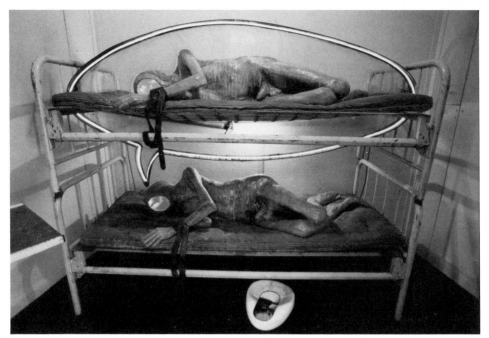

56. Edward Kienholz, *The State Hospital,* 1966. Mixed media, 8' x 12' x 10'. Collection National-museum, Stockholm, Sweden.

57. Edward Kienholz, *The Wait,* 1964–65. Assemblage and mixed media, 6'8" x 12'4" x 6'6". Collection Whitney Museum of American Art, New York.

major environment of the dying. She sits; her animal bone skull hiding the reality behind the false face of her youth. Choked by bottles containing her history, her life is displayed as objects, mementos, and symbols. On the table are photographs, on the wall is a picture; her life has become her past. *The Wait* is a despairing vision of life completed, but life unfulfilled. She waits now, denied the life she did not have and had once wanted; she waits for the death that will be hers forever. Throughout is the feeling of the obsolete and the useless, the emptiness of life, and the bankrupt symbols of nonevents and nonachievements. She is among the living dead, a victim of the premature age that comes with devitalization and valuelessness.

Another environmental sculptor of ex-cellence is Duane Hanson, whose art is distinguished by the unique way in which he has developed assaultive images. Hanson assaults by intrusion. When you are confronted by his perfectly modeled three-dimensional figures, you are not an observer; you do not merely see them. Instead, they are in *your* space, your room; they have invaded your life. *Accident* (*Ill. 58*) is not an environmental sculpture spread out on the gallery floor. It is you who have pulled over to the side of the road and discovered it. Hanson's *Riot* (*see Ill. 85*) is not on your television screen; it is on your street.

Hanson's environmental sculptures confront with images fashioned out of the American mythology. By placing what otherwise would pass as news, or as banal occurrences, within the context of

58. Duane Hanson, *Accident,* 1967. Polyester, fiberglass, mixed media, motorcycle, life-size. Collection Mr. and Mrs. Robert B. Mayer, Illinois.

59. Leonel Góngora, from the series *The Marquis de Sade in Colombia*, 1963. Mixed media, 11″ x 13″. Courtesy the artist.

60. Leonel Góngora, from the series *The Marquis de Sade in Colombia—Exorcismo*, 1963. Mixed media, 18″ x 37″. Courtesy the artist.

an aesthetic experience, Hanson enables the viewer to reperceive in isolation the faces of our environment.

"In his attempt to identify the forces of death and the spirit of life, Colombian artist Leonel Góngora creates an imagery of the mutilated and the destroyer in his earlier drawings and paintings (see *Ills. 59 and 60*). Here he depicts a world of ravenous avengers, and the victims they devour. These images were motivated by acts of human betrayal, characterizing the denial of life and the substitution of force for human communication. In Góngora's recent work—and the work of a genius it is—figures struggle out of repression and victimization in archetypal fantasies of primal sensuality. They consume each other's sex and pleasures as passionately as the earlier images rejected them. *Prisoners of Their Passions (Ill. 61)* is disturbing to many viewers because unbridled sexuality is thought to be more offensive than more violent forms of human enslavement.

Góngora has created a growing body of work comprised of a highly personal, diverse iconography that achieves universality while simultaneously specifically commenting on the mythology of Latin American culture. His sensitive line depicts a populated world of figures—innocent but programmed—struggling to find peak moments of pleasure in a world that is barren. In a subtle and unique relationship with the viewer, the victims communicate their silent accusation; the "prisoners" communicate the passionate fulfillment of their humanness.

The macabre sense of disrelation, and perhaps derangement, is evident in Joyce Treiman's paintings. *Anomie (Ill. 62)*, for example, is a surrealistic fantasy of the ennui of American bourgeois family life. The numerous figures have associated with them some revealing trait, exaggerated to the point of disorder. The woman in beads is a baroque re-creation of the highly sophisticated socialite. The figure of the man standing next to her lends a sense of latent violence and macabre sport to the strange ambiance of this painting. In this atmosphere of neurosis, the individual's clothes are more substantial, and possess more personality than the estranged figures themselves.

Treiman's collection of the slightly mad can be contrasted with Ken Bowman's painting *Aunt Hattie and Her Mother and Her Children (Ill. 63)*, another strangely appealing work. Ugly but familiar, the expressions on the faces of this group are blank and uninviting. The eyes have no vitality within; they are only ovals, with pupils of vacuous intent. There are few indications of inner life and character. These products of American life have little to express. The only life we are impressed with is that of the child, who seems caught in an expression of curiosity and fear; he is the little human, who will be conditioned to become the packaged product of the kin around him. The stages of growth, from the child to the old grandma, depict the history of an American family; their lives tell of failure.

Out of Mexico comes the art of José Luis Cuevas, who has a wide reputation as the creator of the sometimes humorous, sometimes macabre world of figures and fantasies that populate his art (*see Ills. 64 and 65*). Cuevas's unique talent is his ability to perceive and capture the adult world through the eyes of childhood. Thus, his images comprise a caricature of a range of humanity frozen in exaggerated postures, and psychic realities which reveal human situations that are universally familiar.

In this context, one turns to the art of

61. Leonel Góngora, from the series *Prisoners of Their Passions,* 1973. Line drawing, 14″ x 11″. Courtesy the artist.

62. Joyce Treiman, *Anomie,* 1969–70. Oil on canvas, 70″ x 70″. Collection Whitney Museum of American Art, New York.

63. Ken Bowman, *Aunt Hattie and Her Mother and Her Children,* 1970. Acrylic polymer and collage on canvas, 43¼″ x 48¼″. Collection University Art Museum, Berkeley, California. Courtesy Tibor de Nagy Gallery, New York.

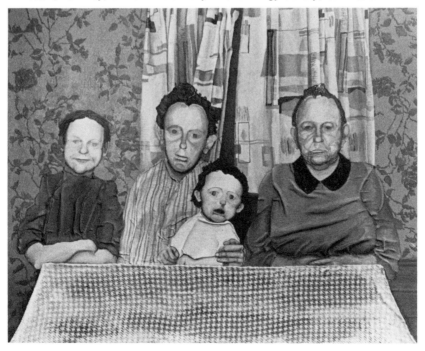

64. José Luis Cuevas, *L'Amour Fou,* 1968. Watercolor on paper, 15½″ x 20½″. Courtesy the artist.

65. José Luis Cuevas, *Police Station.* 1968. Watercolor on paper, 25½″ x 40″. Courtesy the artist.

66. Francis Bacon, *Pope Shouting*, 1951. Oil on canvas, 78″ x 60″. Collection Städtische Kunsthalle, Mannheim.

effective communicators of images of diminished man. Bacon distorts and "diminishes" the Humanistic portrait by Velazquez as a visual statement of the brutality that characterizes our time. This contemporary pope screams out an accusation of his own pain: The protector of mankind is beyond salvation. When compared with the clerical robots of Kinigstein, the satirical figures of Bragg, and the use of Christian imagery in the works of Bermowitz and Landau, Bacon's forceful engagement with the spiritual leader in the twentieth century is revealed to be one of the strongest works created in our time.

This distortion, and the assaultive image that characterized Bacon's earlier works, have since been taken to be the signature of the artist. When his new work was shown in 1968, most of the crit-

John Bratby, an Englishman. Bratby's figures, painted with an Expressionist technique, influenced by Van Gogh, and containing elements of Social Realism and psychic exploration, are among the most haunting depictions of contemporary humanity. The atmosphere of anxiety, the impending sense of collapse that is felt in response to the work, and the ever-present insistence that lives must be better, characterize his work.

Best known among the existential Humanists is another English painter—Francis Bacon. His earlier paintings were outstanding expressions of anger. Paintings like *Pope Shouting* (*Ill. 66*) distinguished the artist years ago as one of the most

67. Francis Bacon. *Two Studies of George Dyer with Dog,* 1968. Oil on canvas, 78″ x 58″. Collection Marlborough Gallery, New York.

68. Ralph Borge, Untitled, 1965. Oil on canvas, 72" x 24". Courtesy the artist.

ics were astonished and disappointed. Critics have a certain impatience with an artist who changes style successfully midstream in his career. They are required to recategorize the artist, and revise past theory. They become confused and angry.

The difference between Bacon's earlier style and his newer work is that he has internalized brutality within the new figures. Moving from the creation of an assaultive, provocative image to a softer, more passive, disturbed image, Bacon has decided not to merely come out to the viewer, but to bring the viewer in. His emotional stance has become less angry and more sorrowful. Despair can be seen as long-term anger.

Works like *Two Studies of George Dyer with Dog* (*Ill. 67*), create an atmosphere of detachment. Perhaps in search of a more personal content, Bacon uses those around him as his models. The forms of their environments, and their relationship to them, give expression to the work. Bacon now communicates by the displacement of the figure in space what he communicated in earlier images with figures greatly distorted by stress. The older images exploded; the new images implode. They are emotive experiences of the inability to place oneself within the world. The figures' positions do not achieve positive relationship to their environment.

Bacon's are mood works. One reacts not to overt signs of human pain, but to subtle emotional conflicts and dislocations that are partly created by Bacon's highly effective use of color. The earlier images dealt with man as mass, as matter, as anatomy in stress. The newer figures deal with man as energy, as rhythm, as force. Here, the tension is created by the inability of energy to make meaningful connection with the world in which it exists. Perhaps success has enabled Bacon, like Shahn, Lebrun, and others, to turn to a more individuated, more personally challenging, idiom of expression.

The fully imploding image is given an environmental quality in the unusual paintings of Ralph Borge. In this almost Surrealistic vision of private moments, Borge's canvases involve us with those who are resigned to their monotonous lives. In each canvas, the viewer shares the silent, personal moments in the life of the subject. Each figure is weighted down by an unseen but overpowering burden. In this nightmare of the vacuity of modern life, we see beauty demolished by living.

The body of the woman climbing the stairs in this untitled work (*Ill. 68*) is still capable of life, but her spirit is not. She wears a wedding veil—she was young and happy once—but her movement is tired and depressed. The stairs again! On the floor is the newspaper, a sign that lives continue, yet all around her are the artifacts of her history, her past that is gone. The building deteriorates, as does her life. Throughout is the feeling of valuelessness, purposelessness. Another unfulfilled life running out its days.

The girl sitting by the window is caught in her loneliness (*see Ill. 69*). Surrounded by childhood, by a room that emphasizes her smallness, she sits thinking, fantasizing, remembering. She is possessed with knowing that all the future holds is another day's defeat, another reason for sorrow. Borge's art embodies lives of quiet desperation.

Many existential Humanists explore the forces in the environment that victimize its inhabitants. Ruth Gikow's *Adoration of the Gadget* (*Ill. 70*) presents a mass of humanity surrounded, confused, and oppressed by the products offered as proof of the success of the technological trans-

69. Ralph Borge, Untitled, 1960. Oil on canvas, 47″ x 20½″. Courtesy the artist.

70. Ruth Gikow, *Adoration of the Gadget,* 1969. Oil on canvas, 60″ x 84″. Courtesy the artist.

71. Anthony Martin, *Infernal Spring of '70,* 1970. Oil on canvas, 52″ x 57″. Courtesy the artist.

formation of society. This anonymous mass exists with their objects, without relationship to one another, without purpose. They are killing time, using their possessions as distractions from the gnawing emptiness. Anthony Martin symbolizes this process by creating generalized rituals of work and death, of destruction and body removal. In *Infernal Spring of '70 (III. 71)* we see a murky atmosphere, in which the animal-man creature directs the body count, much like a grocer takes inventory. In other paintings, Martin gives us a vision of humankind reduced to vegetable existence. No longer the special creation of God, mankind is merely one species in a world of natural forces, interacting without choice, but in the rituals of existence. Robert Broderson creates a similar experience by seeing man metamorphosed into animal creatures (*see III. 72*). Both Martin and Broderson, like Ionesco, with his image of the rhinoceros, see men as betrayers of their potential, who have acquired the identity of a lesser form of life by their actions.

Miriam Beerman, like Martin and Broderson, creates a relationship between nature and humankind. *Bloody Heads (III. 73)*, an early work, is a strong Humanist statement communicating the experience of brutality. Later, the artist created an original iconography, featuring metamorphosed images of man/beast; man turned into merely another creature motivated by the mechanisms of nature. In an interesting reversal, her most recent work seems to suggest that the world of nature is elevating itself, assuming larger than creature status. In her attempt to connect man to forces that make re-

72. Robert Broderson, *Gathering,* 1967. Oil on canvas, 56" x 72". Courtesy Terry Dintenfass, Inc., New York.

newal possible, she has chosen to place nature in man concurrently with man in nature.

Most of these works constitute a challenge to the diversions we use to repress consciousness of the destructive realities of our time. Borge shows how childhood and fantasy can become a refuge from awareness. Peter Walker presents the collapse of order in the frenzy and disruptive pattern of urban life (see *Ill. 74*). His paintings are active, filled with forces in motion. The result of the activity is chaos, confusion, and violence. This complete image of the city, motion, hurrying people, comes as a single vision of turmoil, collision, and terror.

Michael Peters, a young Californian, creates metaphorical images of the vacuity of our environment, embodying the emptiness of its human beings (see *Ill.*

75). Though at first his work seems Surrealistic, we later see these figures as representative shells of human beings that replace living flesh in this architectonic new world. In *Waking Up Beneath Blankets* (*Ill. 76*), Peters shows us the "hard rain" Bob Dylan tells us is going to fall. Dripping its corrosive liquid splash, spilling onto the canvas, it is unnoticed by the dissected and dismembered humanity that sits engaged in what is euphemistically called small talk.

Humanism is the search for a man-centered spirituality. If these images are distorted, transformed, metamorphosed, and mutilated, it is signification of the crucifixion of modern man. These images constitute a myth of despiritualized humanity. They imply that it is not God, but "Man," who must live again. But the resurrection of mankind is a possibility

73. Miriam Beerman, *Bloody Heads,* 1969. Oil on paper collage, 26" x 36". Courtesy the artist.

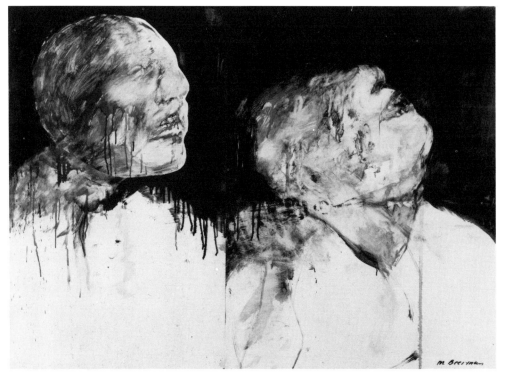

74. Peter Walker, *Blockbuster,* 1968. Acrylic, 8' x 12'. Courtesy Terry Dintenfass, Inc., New York.

75. Michael Peters, *Lavender Mends Dolls and Little Girls' Hearts—Another City Success Story,* 1971. Dyes, colored graphite, and ink, 30" x 40". Courtesy the artist.

76. Michael Peters, *Waking Up Beneath Blankets,* 1971. Dyes, colored graphite, and ink, 30″ x 34″. Courtesy the artist.

contingent on human choice. The possibility of salvation would be still more remote, were there not an art that addressed itself to the diminished state of human spirituality.

Political Humanism

Because a negative critique of the technological society is also, by implication, a rejection of the political establishment that directs it, all Humanist art is, to some degree, political. A political establishment is a mentality infused with power. Insofar as the Humanist artist creates myths, icons, and images that oppose and undermine the prevailing mentality,

his art will be judged as "political" by various power interests.

A number of Humanists feature specific political issues as subject matter in their art. They want to communicate the social awarenesses they believe necessary for political action and social change. Through their art, they wish to contact feelings of another's oppression, and to inspire renewed dedication to the struggle to change society. Because of the concretely political nature of this work, I have chosen, for convenience, to consider it apart from other forms of Humanism.

Unlike the existential Humanist, who expresses anger at the universal dilemma of modern man, the political Humanist relates cause and effect. His is an attack on the institutions and social systems that are responsible for the manipulation and betrayal of man. His perspective is that of the disenfranchised and the oppressed; specific grievances are central to his art.

The political Humanist knows that formalism has influenced more than art history. In contrast to the words and categories of sociology, and the other disciplines concerned with social change, the political Humanist makes clearly identifiable judgments about institutions and social norms. By doing so, he reveals the valuelessness predominant in other approaches to the study of man. His communication is not intended to create reform; he knows that images alone do not change the actions of men. But he also knows that there can be no change without the rejection of existing structures, and without images that support struggle.

The old debate about political art and propaganda no longer holds our interest. As Jacques Ellul has pointed out, there can be no propaganda today without mass media, and little else with it. One wonders even if it is possible to create effective propaganda in an environment already saturated with the programming of the middle class life, consumerism, the American Dream, and technological optimism. Further, the ways in which the art world handles, markets, and exhibits art nullifies the impact of political art. Although art is no longer capable of serving as political propaganda, critics now say that some art is inferior because it is "political." The result, a *political* result, is that within the environment, it is established that art incorporating political concerns or insights is usually considered "bad" art.

Appreciation is based on value judg-ments. If subject matter relating to the struggle to achieve freedom has been rejected, we can only assume that the viewer was not able to handle certain emotions, not that the art is unworthy. Unfortunately, the artist today is subject to many pressures designed to inhibit his enthusiasm for political art. He is told that political art is not universal, that it does poorly on endurance, that it is too limited by specific social situations. In contrast to this formal view is Herbert Marcuse's position that the artist assists the revolution by communicating in a language unsullied by conventional politics. The artist engages in authentic art when "the truth is in the passion and sensibility of the victims of the established order, and not in the executioners."[55]

Political Humanism concerns itself with the "victims of the established order." Artists Ben Shahn, William Gropper, Anton Refrigier, Jack Levine, and Philip Evergood can be mentioned here as the "first generation" of contemporary political Humanists. Their early work dates back to the 1930's, when political art emerged out of a context that was more favorable to its creation. During the three decades since the days of Social Realism and WPA projects, the works of these artists have maintained a consistently high degree of political concern. Their art has been influential in two ways: as statements about the political conditions of our time, and as models for younger artists, who have turned to them for the strength of their convictions as artists, as critical chroniclers of our civilization.

Believing, perhaps, that the social condition determines the human condition, the political Humanists focus on the immediate struggles within the environment. In recent years, their predominant concerns have been with racism and war. Though there has been much discussion of sexism in the art world, this concern has not been widely employed as subject matter. Possibly, by the time this book is published, that situation will have changed.

Perhaps the black artist is the most political of all artists today. The black artist knows that, for three hundred years, America has lied about him. He has seen American society collaborate with racist ideology, and he knows that the structures within the environment, the cultural world, the political establishment, the intelligentsia, and the religious institutions have all rationalized, justified, and cooperated with his physical and psychic enslavement. The black artist does not find it preposterous to suggest that the entire matrix of contemporary aesthetics is a rationale for the displacement of the Humanist artist; he has seen a similar ra-

tionale created within every institution and activity within society for the purpose of excluding him as a human being.

Reginald Gammon is a painter who wants the truth of black history and white oppression to be known. In *Scottsboro Boys (arrest of the nine boys)* (*Ill. 77*), he shows us the helpless victims of white injustice—a universal image of the incarcerated black. In his paintings, we see the victim of injustice made to serve as the cause of his own oppression. Here are universal images of Riker's Island, tenement life, the Tombs, Attica; the prisoner of white society and the victim of white justice. The painting constitutes a portraiture of psychological warfare: the legacy of racism. In *Scottsboro Jury* (*Ill. 78*), the faces of the white jury are concentrated, eyes are directed forward in unchanging gazes. In contrast, the be-

77. Reginald Gammon, *Scottsboro Boys* (*arrest of the 9 boys—March 26, 1931*), 1969. Acrylic on canvas, 36″ x 48″. Courtesy the artist.

78. Reginald Gammon, *Scottsboro Jury,* 1970. Acrylic on canvas, 36″ x 48″. Courtesy the artist.

wildered black faces tell of incomprehension and resignation. These are images of defeat through the legal process. The whiteness of the jury's clothes gives substance and power to these men, while the black men are compressed, herded together like cattle, standing meek and impotent against the forces that will defeat them. The sensitivity of the artist towards these men is strikingly demonstrated in the specificity of the faces of the black men. They are identifiable personalities, with thoughts and feelings that can be contacted, a telling contrast to the anonymity of the white men, whose stonelike faces give no sign of emotion.

A contrast to the images of the Scottsboro Boys is the muscular, proud figure of the self-possessed black, which is Gammon's statement on the *Harlem on My Mind (Ill. 79)* exhibition that was held at New York's Metropolitan Museum of Art. Many black artists protested the show, believing that its images of black people coincided with those of the Scottsboro boys, and not with images of black pride and black consciousness. The white version of the black is the image of the weak and powerless. Here, Gammon places the image of the fighter Jack Johnson over the exhibition of passive images, as a symbol of the continuing struggle of black people.

The burden of black consciousness is strongly revealed in the art of Russ Thompson. In *America, America (Ill. 80),* Old Glory waves overhead, dominating the picture. Below, a smaller, torn Old Glory comes close to the head of James Baldwin, one of the most articulate explicators of the insanity of racism. Baldwin is not the warrior, but the Humanist; not the black avenging angel, or the jive mau mau; not the revolutionary, but the artist. Baldwin is seen to be suffering from the pain of both the conventional image of Old Glory and its torn, exposed reality; the reality that eventually led him to exile.

One might expect the black artist, whose work is political, to choose an art of revenge—an art of black strength overpowering white decadence. But, in fact, among the black artists are many Humanists, whose final statement is an encompassing and moving vision of a world in which racism victimizes everybody, a world where there are no winners and no losers, but only diminished human beings.

Artist and activist Faith Ringgold creates works that are consistent in their

79. Reginald Gammon, *Harlem on My Mind,* 1968. Painting of The Young Jack Johnson. Acrylic on canvas, 32″ x 24″, superimposed on photograph of the Metropolitan Museum of Art, New York. Courtesy the artist.

80. Russ Thompson, *America, America,* 1968. Acrylic collage on Masonite, 50″ x 48″. Collection Ralph Loewy.

exploration of this theme. In *Die* (*Ill. 81*), we see the universal madness of racism, which victimizes everyone. Surrounded by violence, and the insane activity of destruction, the young white and black children are seen huddled together in fear of the brutality around them. At first, *Die* appears to be a conflict of black and white, but soon we see, in the anguished faces, an incredulousness that transcends racial lines to reveal the ritual of destruction. In *The Flag Is Bleeding* (*Ill. 82*),

again we see the flag as the conventional image for America. No longer the symbol of freedom, democracy, and human potential, it has become bloodstained reality of black and white America. The images of black and white are encased by the lines of the flag, which become bars. While the figures of black and white are joined by clasping arms, the black man is holding a knife. It is he who has stabbed the flag; it is black people, implies the artist, who are leading the strug-

81. Faith Ringgold, *Die,* 1967. Oil on canvas, 6′ x 12′. Courtesy the artist.

82. Faith Ringgold, *The Flag is Bleeding,* 1967. Oil on canvas, 6′ x 8′. Courtesy the artist.

gle against the oppression that affects everyone. While the joining of the two whites and the black would seem to symbolize hope, and the possibility of coming together, the black is isolated and separated from the rest by the stars of the flag; they are his death mask. The three are linked by a common oppression, and are, at the same time, separated by the extent of their responses to it.

Ringgold's style is a conscious attempt to evoke the reductiveness of African art. Only the necessary forms are delineated, in order to describe basic passions. Ringgold's works are "simple," straightforward, and employ an iconography designed to have the most direct communicable impact.

Another painter whose work is largely about the experience and consequences of racism is Cliff Joseph. In *The Superman* (*Ill. 83*), Joseph combines the imagery of white supremacy with the myths that have for so long kept it alive. The skeletal figure of the superman is adorned with his implements: the cross, the hangman's rope, the matches for the burning. In place of genitalia, there is a militarist's medal. There is also the gun, whip, and rifle. Revealed here is the creature who would enslave, brutalize, pervert, and conduct psychic warfare for economic gain. Now burdened by his weapons, devoid of life, we see the decadent figure dying.

In *He Has Long White Chain On* (*Ill. 84*), Benny Andrews paints the powerful image of black America chained in its struggle to be free. The image of freedom exists as a shadow; no longer held by chains, the shadow is powerful and dynamic. The actual figure is strained and held immobile. The painting style, typical of Andrews and several other black artists, is conspicuously primitive. Andrews

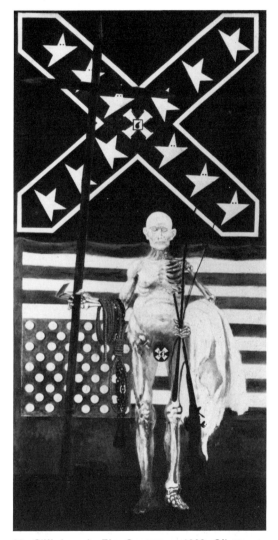

83. Cliff Joseph, *The Superman,* 1966. Oil on Masonite, 48" x 24". Courtesy the artist.

84. Benny Andrews, *He Has Long White Chain On,* 1966. Oil on canvas, 50" x 50". Courtesy the artist.

85. Duane Hanson, *Riot,* 1968. Fiberglass, polyester, mixed media, life-size. Courtesy the artist.

86. Mahler Ryder, *The Great American Tool (-up) and Die,* 1971. Ink on paper, 23″ x 30″. Courtesy the artist.

feels his content so intensely, he deals only with the essential communication of struggle, and is not preoccupied with providing relief for the viewer's eye.

The background of the painting is a psychological landscape of the imprisoned man, sparse and bare. Only by freeing himself can the black man find other environments. Andrews has created the black Sisyphus; one with the possibility of freedom through rebellion against the white gods.

The universal madness of racism, and its pervasive influence, is the experience of Duane Hanson's *Riot* (*Ill. 85*). Here is a work focused on the American ritual of brutality. The symbol of America here is not the flag, but the cop. He is dressed in the "uniform" that symbolizes the legitimacy of the system, the same system that tried the Scottsboro boys. To witness Hanson's *Riot* is to discover that no aspect of racial conflict is anything but bestial. Racism is the rot of human values; anything that gives it life is evil.

Mahler Ryder, a black artist, converts the cop to the construction worker (*see Ill. 86*); conservative, middle-American, redneck, unthinking pawn in the game, equipped with a hand of steel, of nuts and bolts. His face is obscure, his eyes hidden by his glasses. This is the black vision of the white American male, the black-hater, and the man metamorphosed into an unthinking, malicious machine.

Other artists, black and white, are more interested in the exploration of the system that perpetuates racism than in the images of exploiters and victims. The cop, the politician, the servant of the system—those who bring to the insanity of human exploitation the sanction of legality and legitimacy—are frequent images found within political Humanist art. These images of law and order, of law enforcers, of functionaries, are found throughout

87. Jack Levine, *The Feast of Pure Reason,* 1971. Aquatint mezzotint, 19⅜" x 25". Courtesy the artist.

the work of Joseph Hirsch, Jack Levine, and John Dobbs. They are usually presented as figures with little definition; the implication is that they are devoid of individual motivation and identity. They are servants of a larger compulsion: the soldiers, the national guardsmen, who do not question why. The death of the self is required for service as the arm of the law. The uniformity of these figures as politicians, as policemen, as bureaucrats, is reinforced by the sameness of their outer garments; a suggestion that the outward appearance is indicative of an inner uniformity, as well. The environments into which these figures are placed are dreary and empty; only the central direct action is spotlighted—the blind and passionless function of these selfless men.

Jack Levine's art can be partially characterized by images of situations of victimization. In *The Feast of Pure Reason* (*Ill. 87*), Levine brings the cop together with the stuffed and decadent, overfed and overdressed politician. *The Feast of Pure Reason* is testimony to their collusion. Pure reason, the insanity of the "rational" system, places authority in the hands of fools, and guns in the hands of their unthinking servants. The atmosphere of the work is black, amorphous, and indistinct. Levine's compressed imagery, and the enclosing background, create the feeling of threat, the danger of the self-righteous and the "responsible."

The Trial (*Ill. 88*), although painted between 1953 and 1954, serves as a remarkably relevant image for many of the most important political issues that have since inspired conscience and conflict in America. The Chicago Conspiracy Trial, Angela Davis, Huey Newton, the Berrigan brothers, Eldridge Cleaver, H. Rap Brown; over the past ten years, the courts have been used as a political weapon to imprison, to dissipate energy, and to exile. In this powerful painting, Levine creates the feeling of the drab, pretentious, and uninspired legal process. The painting has a quality of baroque ornamentation, an implication of decadence and lost purpose, a feeling of predictable outcomes, and a sense of lethargic deliberation. The compressed imagery, the distorted faces,

the organization of the figure on the canvas, all suggest that each figure is a small part of an organic whole, each a functionary in a predetermined activity. It is more a beehive with its workers, its hierarchies, and its queen—the judge—overseeing all action.

John Dobbs's *Media Image* (*Ill. 89*) presents the lawmaker in his public posture. Here, Dobbs creates a bestial imagery of vice and corruption. The lawmaker, the politician, become spokesmen for the forces of death. This is an assemblage, a compressed image of the thousands of images that besiege us daily. Here is the method for every campaign, every

88. Jack Levine, *The Trial,* 1953–54. Oil on canvas, 72″ x 63″. Collection The Art Institute of Chicago.

speech, every lie. The work indicts the political game and the betrayals that are inevitable. We see the multiple images of those who seek power and misuse human life.

Speech is translated into program in Dobbs's *Deodand #2* (*III. 90*). We are presented with the summary image of the enforcer. His most outstanding appendage is his gun, pointed at you, the viewer. It is a static image that conveys manic energy. Here is Kent State, Vietnam, Southern justice, and Northern law and order. It is the image of what is necessary to keep the peace. The cop, like an absurd caricature of a football hero, has his humanity submerged by his helmet. His features are obscure. Only his gun and his shooting eye are visible. Fixed in the act of killing, he represents all those who have converted law into an exercise of coercion. The experience of threat is intensified as Dobbs minimizes the distance between the viewer—the potential victim—and the nozzle of the gun.

The art of Juan Genovés creates metaphysical encounters of the enforcers and their victims. In the portfolio of prints entitled *Silencio, Silencio* (*see III. 91*), we are witness to authorized force and indiscriminate killing. Genovés's use of undetailed silhouettes creates an atmosphere of anonymity, filled with the threat of senseless brutality in the time of mass man. Undefined and unnamed, granted the power to uphold peace and order at all costs, these authorities wield their weapons without discretion. The multiple images, presented in temporal and spatial sequence, intensify the frenzy and panic. Genovés's style, a highly refined and calculated understatement, forces the viewer to take caution for his own life; that street may be his own, those victims may include himself. The force of evil

89. John Dobbs, *Media Image,* 1968. Oil on canvas, 74″ x 38″. Courtesy the artist.

90. John Dobbs, *Deodand #2,* 1969. Oil on canvas, 40″ x 36″. Courtesy A.C.A. Gallery, New York.

91. Juan Genovés, *Afterwards, with the Ones Before,* from the *Silencio, Silencio* portfolio, 1970. Aquatint, 19¾″ x 26″. Courtesy Marlborough Graphics, New York.

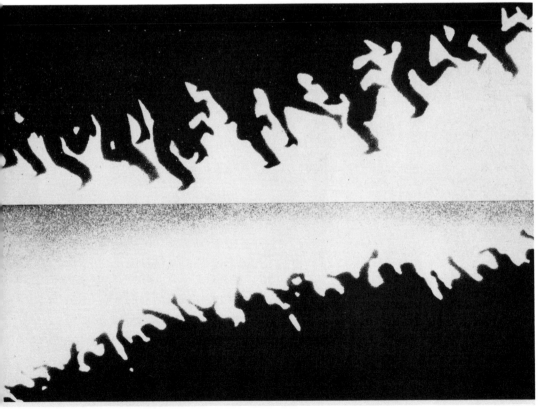

92. Joseph Hirsch, *Triptych*, 1967–69. Oil on canvas, 5' x 10'. Courtesy Forum Gallery, Inc., New York.

must be dealt with before we run from his bullets. Genovés has created a unique expression: a generalized political art.

In *Triptych (Ill. 92)*—a summary statement of the experience of American political life—Joseph Hirsch presents the scenario of a decade of political conflict. Mad dogs, cops in gas masks resembling robotic humanity, the bystanders—young, guitar-laden, flower-powered, disenfranchised—the technology of the prowl car, the ironically situated, anachronistic cannon and cannonballs; all of these comprise the environment and the content of the painting. It is not a moving work; it is a disturbing one. Here is the crunch of modern life. The polluted environments are cleansed by the instruments of law; monochromatic, devoid of joy, technological in feeling, irrational in action, despiritualized in essence. The *Triptych* is both a characteristic Hirsch, and an important painting.

Many of the works of political Humanists deal with the nature of war. The political Humanist does not agonize over the merits of war. Instead, he wishes to raise consciousness and indignation at

93. Chaim Koppelman, *Vietnam,* 1965. Aquatint, 19¾″ x 15¾″. Courtesy the artist.

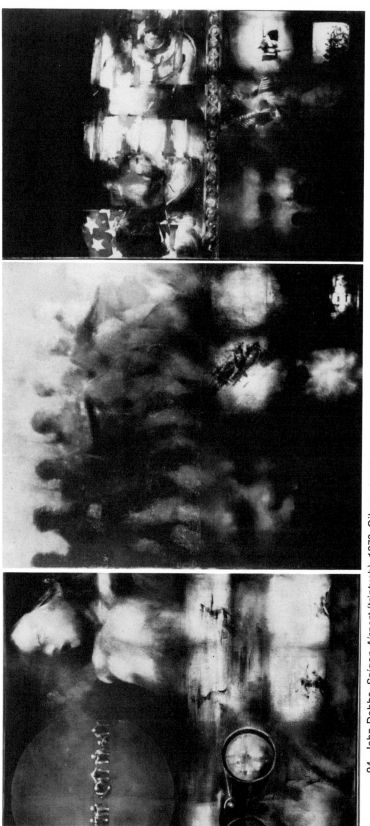

94. John Dobbs, *Saigon Airport* (triptych), 1970. Oil on canvas.
Left panel: *Arrival*, 54" x 36"; center panel: *Presence*, 54" x 46";
right panel: *Departure*, 54" x 36". Collection Roy R. Neuberger, New York.

what is done in our name. Unlike the paltry exercises of modernists who have on occasion lifted their brushes in political statements, the political Humanists have consistently kept before us images of death by militarized technology. Although the works do not capture the intensity of war itself, as works of art they are disturbing experiences. We can ignore the images of the war-mutilated when they are presented as "news," but we are less able to dismiss them when they are the result of the artistic choice to make these images part of our aesthetic experience.

Clearly, one possible option for a sensitive person today is to expose the reality of war by demanding that society live with images of the consequences of its inhumanity. Perhaps, if mutilated human beings are our art, we will be less willing to create them in life.

Unlike Baranik's image of the Vietnamese infused with strength and dignity, the figure in Chaim Koppelman's *Vietnam* (*III. 93*) conveys only holocaust. Scorched and violated humanity is expressed through the image of the dead child, and the numbed shock of its parent. The rough and eroded surface of the work evoke the charred humanity who are the victims of war. The work makes all ideological reasons and political rationalizations for war only words to cover the gross barbarism of our acts. As long as dead men are body counts, and heroism is defined as senseless murder, we deserve an art that reminds us of our crimes.

John Dobbs's triptych, *Saigon Airport* (*III. 94*), expresses the totality of the Vietnam war. We see the soldiers who take lives; we see innocent victims, symbolized by the baby; we *feel* the experience of running from gun shots fired from trees or houses. We feel eyes watching us, and gun sights lowered towards us,

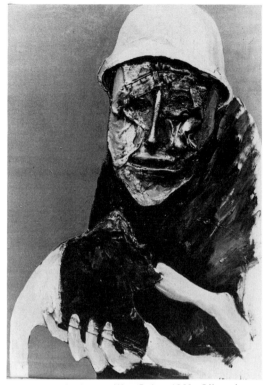

95. Benny Andrews, *War Baby,* 1968. Oil and collage, 35″ x 25″. Courtesy the artist.

and we recognize the propagandistic ideology which perpetuates this insanity. It is the hysterical, senseless, brutal barbarism of an inane war, expressed with an outrage created by paint on canvas.

Benny Andrews's concern with children and war is painfully revealed in *War Baby* (*III. 95*). The image is clear: The child's legs are seen to be withered and skeletal; it lies dead in the hands of a soldier, whose face is metamorphosed into bronze, wire, metal, rivets, and cold steel. His emotion is bewilderment; he will remain frozen in that posture, but it will not bring life to the dead. He has killed, but cannot understand death, nor the consequence of his participation.

Peter Passuntino elevates the image

of the child-death to a symbolic level in *War Birth* (*III. 96*). We see birth in our century as an act of destruction and death. The pain of labor is no longer joyful; now it is the ritualized expulsion of fated humanity. The death of fertility, and the potential as sacrifice to the gods of war, cause mothers to produce skeletal children. Canger's painting, *Birth* (*see III. 34*), like Passuntino's, is the vision of the creation of the doomed. In Canger's painting, however, the newly created is excrement; in Passuntino's, it is death.

Central to any discussion of political Humanism is the work of Edward Kienholz. In *The Portable War Memorial* (*III. 97*), Kienholz has created an environmental sculpture that serves as a practical reminder of the more violent aspect of the American character. The work is designed to be incorporated into any suitable space. Because war is an everyday feature of our lives, because it fills our media, takes our sons, is our news, and accounts for our greatest commitment of resources, why shouldn't it be present in our homes and gathering places? The artist suggests this idea by placing the

96. Peter Passuntino, *War Birth,* 1969. Ink, chalk, and watercolor, 14" x 14". Courtesy the artist.

97. Edward Kienholz, *The Portable War Memorial*, 1968. Mixed media, 9½′ x 8′ x 32′. Collection Kunst- und Museumbibliothek der Stadt Köln.

war memorial in the context of a hot dog and chili stand. Here is the gesture of victory after battle, the raising of the symbol of freedom, the vision of Iwo Jima as "everybattle," alongside the frivolity of our daily lives. We see the woman in the garbage can, underemphasized and ironic in terms of the heroic action set before us. We see the draft poster, calling for more youths to add to the rosters of dead heroes. The couple at the hot dog stand sit and enjoy their plastic food, indifferent to the realities to which the memorial alludes. Apathetic, unconscious, hand in hand, they live on, with perverted visions of masculinity, violence, and victory.

Edward Kienholz is the Goya of three-dimensional space. He, too, has a vision of the underbelly of life. His work is a cryptic revelation of what we are about; he gives form and substance to our myths.

The decision to create political Humanism is not made lightly; the artist knows there is a certain amount of risk involved. He knows that, of all the kinds of art created today, political art is least likely to be exhibited, appreciated, bought, written about, and supported. Yet, when the

inclusion of political awarenesses comes as a logical step in the development of the artist's work, the artist is compelled to follow the work to where it seems to want to go.

The process through which a painter moves from a personal, naturalistic style to a mature political Humanism can be traced in a discussion of the work of May Stevens. The political nature of her recent canvases is attributable to personal exploration and growth as an artist. The starting point for the progression of her political art is seen in paintings like *The Living Room* (*Ill. 98*). Here, Stevens is concerned with an autobiographical Daddy. "He was a relative of mine," the artist tells us. "The man in the portrait represented to me an authoritarianism and a closed attitude toward the world which was something that disturbed me very, very much. It was a middle American attitude towards culture, towards politics, towards black people, towards Jews, the whole works, the whole syndrome, a closed, isolated life."[56]

The development of the artist's painting led to the elevation of "Daddy" to

"Big Daddy," a more universal image of these qualities of the American identity. "Big Daddy" is the image of authoritarianism in America, first expressed in a redundant satire featuring "Big Daddy" and his animal incarnation, the bulldog. Affected by the past decade of turmoil, and influenced by the logical development of the work, Stevens turned from an enigmatic imagery to a symbolic political painting. Satire is often an indirect expression of anger, and it is anger that emerges in *Big Daddy Paper Doll* (*Ill. 99*). This painting, and others like it, are examples of a mature political Humanism. Though Stevens is well aware of the dangers involved in the creation of political Humanism, her work is clearly validated by the integrity of the process by which it came to be achieved.

Big Daddy Paper Doll is a refutation of the belief that politics in art leads to propaganda. This large painting is a step in a progressive direction of creating an art that comes to terms with all of the aspects of the environment that are responsible for the diminution of human values. We must accept the images of the racist, the militarist, the executioner, the cop, and "Big Daddy," as well as the allegorical, blood-stained synthesis of all the images. They are not political posi-

98. May Stevens, *The Living Room*, 1965. Oil on canvas, 64" x 81". Courtesy the artist.

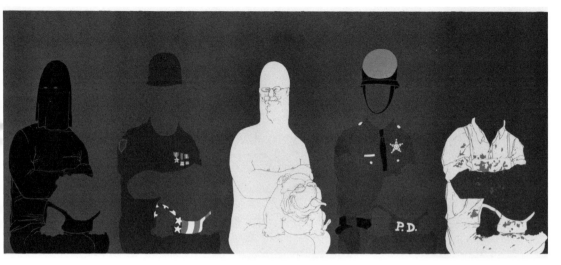

99. May Stevens, *Big Daddy Paper Doll,* 1969. Acrylic, 6' x 14'. Courtesy the artist.

tions or ideological representations; they are the most external faces of what were, for the artist, internal awarenesses, first expressed in the intimacy of a highly personal expression. The development from autobiographical narrative painting to abstract, and then specific, satire, and then to mature political imagery, assures that Stevens's political Humanism will be seen as a result of the progressive sophistication of her intention, and not as political clichés.

Obviously, the work of political Humanists is not blessed (or cursed) by widespread acceptance. It is not an art that caters to the clearly articulated needs of collectors, critics, and gallery owners. John Dobbs's dealer once told him that visitors to the gallery liked his work, but wouldn't buy it, because they didn't want to hang his paintings in their homes. Dobbs then built a canvas with an attached door, so that, when the purchaser received guests in his home, he could close the door, and hide the painting.

The Absurdists

There are moments in a man's life when he feels a curious detachment from his environment. At such times, a chuckle begins to grow inside him. The chuckle gets louder and louder, and, finally, bursts forth as tumultuous laughter. In one split second, the entire absurdity of life, man, and society has filled his psyche. Instantaneously, he realizes that his behavior, and that of his neighbors, is based on the most absurd of motivations. The forms of existence have no justification: Life is a hoax, and the structures of modern life a hoax within a hoax. For the absurd Humanists, this moment is forever.

These Humanists reveal the dual absurdity. Man himself, and absurd man living with the illusion of rationality. The absurd Humanists want to dismantle the dominant value system of society. Their target is all that has come to be considered "normal," those values and modes of behavior we find tolerable or acceptable, that we legitimize by taking seriously. The absurdist, in his most extreme moments, feels so alienated from society that he observes those around him as one would look upon another species: a similar form of life, but so different in orientation and basic values, so fundamentally motivated by insanity and destructiveness, that it must be classified as something substantially different from human.

This feeling of another's inhumanity is an artistic impulse, not a moral one. The artist does not see himself in a superior position. He is as much the victim of contemporary absurdity as he is its depictor. Several artists respond to what they see by satire, by ridiculing the existing forms of behavior. Others create utterly outrageous fantasies, which are still no more insane than those we possess already. Still a third kind of absurdist tries to embarrass us, with exaggeration of the fantasies he believes we already have.

The absurdists, more than other Humanists, are specifically "American" artists. Their images are concretely rooted in the American experience, and it is they who have created new forms of this kind of Humanism. While other artists have debated the problems and possibilities of creating multiple images on the canvas, the absurdists have plunged ahead to create a fresh and original art that leaves formal conventions behind. Peter Dean has been compelled to build extensions to his canvas to accommodate the figures spilling off of them. Jay Milder, Alan Bermowitz, Philip Sherrod, and others create works which barely contain the crowded dynamic humanity enclosed by the frames. Cartoonists like S. Clay Wilson, Spain Rodriguez, and Robert Crumb have definitively developed the cartoon format to a new sophistication. The absurdists have shown us that many of the

questions raised by art critics concerning the rendering of the human figure, or groups of figures, were largely academic. Their work demonstrates that the problem of the figure is not a formal one, but arises because many artists are unable to decide *what to do with the figure*—the problem of content.

Perhaps the most important innovation to be found here is the development of a new access and distribution system for absurd Humanism. While other artists complain about the dealer system, the precious object, and the compromises necessary for success, the cartoonists on the West Coast have created a new format, and a massive audience for their work. They have remade the comic book into one of the most effective forms of visual communication, and, by doing so, have granted themselves unlimited possibilities for the exploration of content.

However the absurdists accomplish their intention, the outcome of their efforts is unmistakable: The insanity of what passes as sane is undeniably revealed. One cannot easily slip back into the "routine"; one can no longer function unconsciously. Through the work of the absurdists, one comes to feel that the workings of social custom, political ideology, consumerism, social values, and social roles are irrational, without human justification, unnecessary, and often destructive.

Like most absurdists, the artist Marisol satirizes existing social norms. She creates *The Party* (*Ill. 100*), a gathering of friends to share in a communal evening of companionship and joy, but shows us, by exaggeration and insight, the typical encased and isolated beings who are, in Auden's term, "unknown citizens." Their clothes are boxes that hide their bodies. Their faces are masks that hide their private worlds. They are together, this assemblage of people, but they are alone, and incapable of connection. Immobile and uncommunicative, they exist in an elegantly fashionable surround that is the coffin of contemporary sociality. The cocktail party, the opening, the convention reception—these are the death worlds of automated social situations.

June Leaf, whose work has influenced more than a few Humanists, satirizes a particular social interaction, or lack of it, in her created experience of social/sexual roles. The *Tin Theater* (*III. 101*) is a baroque entertainment box of the universal degradation of men and women in that social game once called "courtship," and today called "making it." The more passive image of the woman is contrasted with the overdynamic, manipulative bi-

cycle-riding man. The work itself produces music, and the figures endlessly circle in their locked-in roles. On this stage, this puppet theater suggestive of life itself, we see the same encapsulated experience found in Marisol. It is the private drama of manipulation and submission, of conformity to the social pressures of the environment.

Ralph Massey, a talented California sculptor, creates a satirical portraiture of programmed people and debased values. His images convey the conditioned human beings who have reified their values. In their ridiculousness, these characters give human reality to myths which are taken very seriously, but which are fundamentally absurd. *Stand Up and Be Counted* (*III. 102*) is a mythic vision of the plastic, fleshy men and women so-

100. Marisol, *The Party,* 1965–66. Mixed media, 9'11" x 15'8" x 16'. Collection Mr. and Mrs. Robert B. Mayer, Illinois. Courtesy Sidney Janis Gallery, New York.

ciety has taken as its image of youth. "Love it or leave it," but don't turn around and find each other.

In *The Last American Art* (*Ill. 103*), we see demonstrated every home-body's fantasy of making pornography on a Sunday afternoon. Here is the American fantasy of fulfillment, Massy's contemptuous and satirical art spotlights the fixtures in American dreams. In *The Sirens* (*Ill. 104*), we see the species grown older, double images, inseparable and thinking similar thoughts, appearing in chairs on the porch, in old age homes, in institutions. They watch America pass by, as they move their jowly jaws in judgment. Fleshy, fat, indifferent, and without vitality, they are burdened by their own weight. All these figures are without pleasure; the couple that faces some higher allegiance,

101. June Leaf, *Tin Theater,* 1969. Wood frame covered by olive cans painted over with figures (motorized construction—illuminated by electric lights), 82″ x 28″ x 27″. Detail above right. Collection Mr. and Mrs. Herbert Lust, Illinois.

102. Ralph Massey, *Stand Up and Be Counted,* 1969. Lacquered terra-cotta and Plexiglas, 36″ x 15″ x 15″. Collection Mr. and Mrs. Nat Freedland.

103. Ralph Massey, *The Last American Art,* 1970. Lacquered terra-cotta and Plexiglas, 57″ x 25″ x 11″. Collection Mr. Ben Bencort.

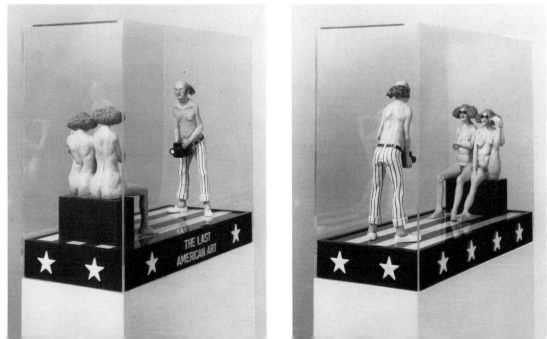

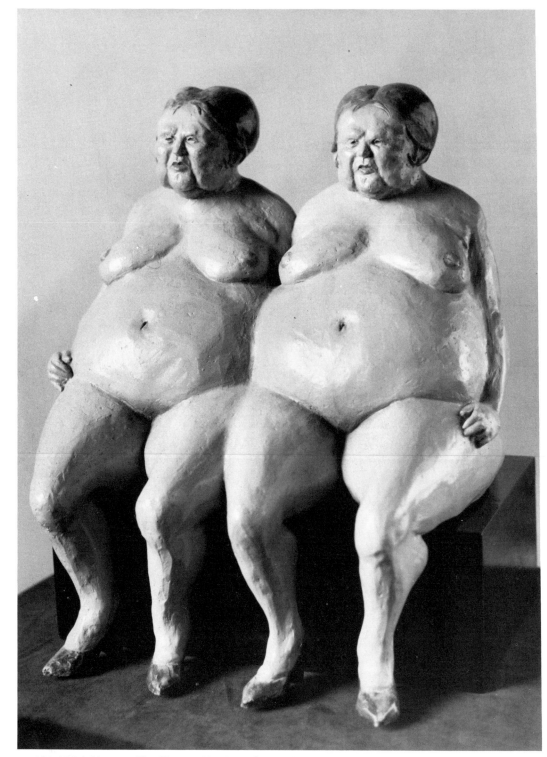

104. Ralph Massey, *The Sirens,* 1967. Polyester, resin, and fiberglass, 21″ x 17″ x 13″. Collection Judge Nicholas J. Lambros.

the fat old figures of fatigued sensuality, and the burlesque of sexuality in the peep show porno.

Twisted values and vacuous myths are subject matter for sculptor Luis Jimenez. In *Barfly and Old Woman* (*III. 105*), we see the young and sensuous woman wasted by the farce of sex appeal and patriotism. In Jimenez's mockery of American values, the Statue of Liberty has been transformed into a cheapened plastic object for entertainment; now she is a display embodying contemporary American values. She is watched by her future, the aged woman who sits, possessing less life than the cat which is perched on her lap.

Many of the works created by May Stevens demonstrate a sophisticated absurdist vision (*see III. 106*). Stevens creates images that are cool and detached. Her content is utterly irrational, but, on first appearance, seems perfectly normal and acceptable. It is the viewer who becomes scandalized, when he discovers that what he had initially accepted as perfectly natural is a grotesque parody of values. Stevens's absurd Humanism makes us painfully aware of how many thoroughly inane assumptions are made daily by those who wish to function smoothly in an environment fraught with perverted and corrupt definitions of human and social relationships.

105. Luis Jimenez, *Barfly,* 1970. Fiberglass and epoxy, 7' high; *Old Woman with Cat,* 1969. Fiberglass and epoxy, 3' high. Courtesy the artist.

106. May Stevens, *Big Daddy Robed,* 1971. Acrylic, 80″ x 72″. Courtesy the artist.

107. Sidney Chafetz, *Newly Elected,* 1970. Intaglio on zinc, 11⅞″ x 13¾″. Courtesy the artist.

If Massey's images are of people who have succumbed to the ideology of the American value structure, Stevens's figures are the incarnate values, themselves. In both cases, there is no self-consciousness in the images. They are images of people who do not doubt themselves, do not question the self-righteousness that possesses them.

The art of printmaker Sidney Chafetz consists of satirical civiscapes. In *Newly Elected* (*Ill. 107*), Chafetz conveys the "do-gooders," the middle-aged matrons who are embossed with "civic" responsibility. They sit like nails in the coffin of community life, erect and stern. Although the detailing of each character is minimal, the presence of self-righteous, arrogant, and self-assured human beings permeates the intaglio print.

Another vision of the absurd protec-tors of the public good is to be found in the ritualized guardians created by Edward Schlinski. The angry, rabid dog, and his lunatic master, welcome with their fangs (*see Ill. 108*). Their mode of existence is raw violence, threat, and intimidation. They are the guardians of " 'Big Daddy's' Domain." But, in sculptured form, and with a specific exaggeration, they stand out as totems, mocking, not exemplifying, the customs of America. Charles Bragg, another Californian, transforms "Big Daddy" into a comedy of absurd authority (*see Ill. 109*). Here, the general lies on his side, ever mindful of the position of the flag, a victim of programmed mentality to the end. Out of his mind and out of his space, he has succumbed to the artist's parody of his vacuous function.

Behind the bulldog guardian, and the

108. Ed Schlinski, *Figure Study for a proposed monument memorializing man's ascent to primacy over the beasts,* 1970. Papier-mâché and acrylic, 38" high. Collection Mr. and Mrs. Richard Lerner, New York.

mad-dog cop, comes the keeper of the flock himself, satirized by artist Oyvind Fahlström. In *Notes No. 4 (C.I.A. Brand Bananas)* (*Ill. 110*), Fahlström creates a visual foreign policy, a master plan, a major document of the Cold War. Here is the madness of the rituals that characterize foreign affairs. In *Exercise (Nixon)* (*Ill. 111*), Fahlström has the President of the United States give his State of the Human Message. Some will argue that Fahlström's art is an oversimplification, that political questions require a more complex analysis. Sure.

Fahlström's work, like most absurdist art, demystifies experience. It cleanses the mind of the assumptions of legitimacy we confer on many realities that, were we really able to see them, we would find repulsive. Insofar as it helps us to see freshly what we are conditioned not to

see at all, absurd Humanism is an important reference point for the evaluation of contemporary values.

The absurdist vision is brought to the subject of race relations in America by artist Robert Gwathmey. Gwathmey's art is a surgeon's scalpel used to cut to the heart of contemporary values (see *Ill. 112*). Here, the bastion of democracy is unable to overcome the disturbing news that some men have different skin coloring than others. The ritual of the school bus burning, the cotton-picker, the shiftless wino, the Confederate soldier, all serve as backdrops to America's latest "space shot." Gwathmey, conveying the history of the black man in America through the eyes of the absurdist, presents whitey in the space suit, looking like a pig beneath his helmet; this legacy of spiritual corruption looks out into

109. Charles Bragg, *At Ease,* 1969. Etching, 4" x 6". Collection Basil Collier.

110. Oyvind Fahlström, *Notes No. 4* (*C.I.A. Brand Bananas*), 1970. Ink and acrylic on paper, 16½″ x 14″. Courtesy The Museum of Modern Art, New York.

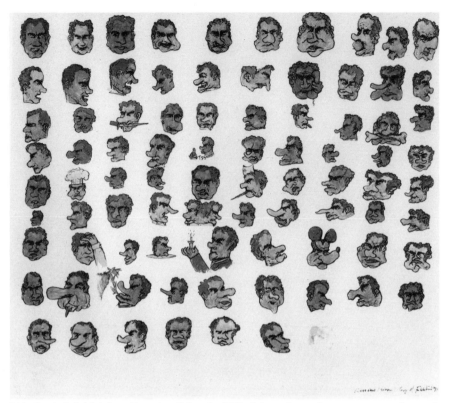

111. Oyvind Fahlström, *Exercise (Nixon),* 1971. Ink and acrylic on paper, 14″ x 16″. Courtesy Sidney Janis Gallery, New York.

112. Robert Gwathmey, *Space,* 1964. Oil on canvas, 36″ x 48″. Collection Mr. and Mrs. Murray Handwerker, New York.

113. Elias Friedensohn, *Diagram Showing Where Bullet Entered the Body of Victim; Diagram Showing How Bullet Was Concealed and His Inner Corruption,* 1964–67. Acrylic, both 40″ x 26″. Courtesy Terry Dintenfass, Inc., New York.

114. Elias Friedensohn, *Interrogation (large),* 1964–67. Acrylic and mixed media, 64½″ x 49″. Courtesy Terry Dintenfass, Inc., New York.

Space, where he wants to bring the insane views he thinks are his contribution to the universe.

Elias Friedensohn re-creates experiences of the universal irrationality of creature-man in country-America in his painting *Diagram Showing Where Bullet Entered the Body of Victim; Diagram Showing How Bullet Was Concealed and His Inner Corruption* (*Ill. 113*). Here, his victim is set up against the American flag. The unknown bystander, a witness, traces the trajectory of the bullet that killed the young President. Confronted with murder, he has a singular interest in physics. The flag is the backdrop for the recurring drama, the struggle for power. In *Interrogation (large)*, (*Ill. 114*), Friedensohn gives us the modern gun, the steeled

115. James Grashow, *Murder Maché* figures, 1969–71. Fiberglass, cloth, polyester resin, approx. 8′ high. Courtesy Allan Stone Gallery, New York.

mass of bureaucracy, the institutional secularization of confession, the black pit of mind-jamming.

Victims and torturers, stripped of the "ideals" that motivate their actions, are, in the end, only irrational men. The work of James Grashow creates this experience in monumental terms. Here, in these *Murder Maché* figures (*Ill. 115*), is a parody of senseless battle; eight-foot figures caught posed in their acts of violence and irrationality. Without issues, without a side to identify with, we are left no other possible experience but to witness the complete absurdity of battle, itself.

Purposeless hate is parodied in the cartoons of Spain Rodriguez and the satire of Alan Bermowitz. Both Bermowitz (*see Ill. 116*) and Spain create the supercop, the hip militarist, the tireless servant and protector of the common good. Spain's *Trashman* (*Ill. 117*) is, of course, no better than those he fights against; the greater threat to human values are the men empowered to protect them. Trashman "fights for freedom," filling the world with the corpses of his enemies. *Tak tak tak tak tak* is a satire on the entire military force approach to the solution of human problems that characterizes the mentality of the political establishment today. But, if Trashman is absurd, he is no more so than the "acceptable," "normal," "common" assumption that social problems are ameliorated by stricter enforcement of existing laws.

Spain's cartoons are fantasies in action. He gives us images that—though grotesque—are no less real than what we normally call reality. An inverted metaphor for the American environment, Trashman *is* law and order. He elects Presidents.

Another approach chosen by some absurd Humanists is the creation of fanta-

116. Alan Bermowitz, Untitled, 1970. Pen and ink, 14″ x 16″. Courtesy the artist.

117. Manuel "Spain" Rodriguez, *Trashman Fights for Freedom*, 1970. Ink on paper, 10″ x 7″. Courtesy the artist.

sies that allow people to become what it would seem they wish to be. Consider Edward Paschke's *M.A. Lady* (*Ill. 118*). She believes in the ideology of America (witness the tattoo); she is the creation of American mythology. She is the hateful killer-bitch given her form of fulfillment; then she is the prizefighter, muscular and fearless, independent and potent, now ready for any opponent. The Statue of Liberty has disrobed, dropped her book and torch, stepped off her island, and entered into the ring of life. *M.A. Lady* is Myra Breckinridge, Marilyn Monroe, the boxer champ, Batman, ski champ, he-man, made into a mythic mix by the artist. He/she is a grotesque, comprised of all the familiar images regarded by most people as natural, acceptable, and even desirable.

Jay Milder, another of the Rhino Horn group, combines Biblical imagery, animal/human metamorphosis, and images of contemporary America in his satirical painting (*see Ill. 119*). Milder finds the same isolation in the subway car that Marisol discovers at *The Party,* but instead of hiding in self-made boxes, Milder's partygoers are metamorphosed into animal humans, oinking, baying, squawking, and grunting at each other the now corrupted wisdom of Western civilization.

118. Edward Paschke, *M.A. Lady,* 1970. Oil on canvas, 72" x 52". Collection Mr. and Mrs. Henry Buchbinder, Illinois.

119. Jay Milder, *Inside the Ark I*, 1970. Oil on canvas, 34" x 24".
Collection Rabbi Malcomb Thompson, Connecticut.

Milder gives old myths new force by incorporating them in allegorical paintings of absurdist intent.

Peter Dean, of the Rhino Horn, re-creates the legends of the American past, and the fantasies of the American imagination, in fantasia worlds of myth and icon. This outstanding young painter crowds his canvases with the bold colors and quintessential imagery of modern America. From the hunter, surrounded by his woman and other *Trophies (Ill. 120)* to the last stand of Custer *(see Ill. 121)*, Dean blows up these myths to gigantic proportions, so that we may begin to question the fantasies we have thought worthy of us.

Dean is aware of the animal in us we choose to ignore; he paints human boredom attacked by instinct, impulse, scream, and insanity. Joseph Hirsch is also aware of the "animalism" of his human contemporaries. Not attacked by fantasy, as they are in Dean's works, Hirsch's figures are guided by raw instinct, unthinking animal passion. *Al Dente (Ill. 122)* is Hirsch's way of satirizing a society that spends literally billions of dollars a year to pretty itself up, to perpetuate the illusion of beauty, and yet appears, because of its actions, as a creature driven by insatiable hunger, gluttonous greed, and manic consumption.

Seymour Rosofsky is another absurdist

120. Peter Dean, *Trophies,* 1971. Oil on canvas, 76″ x 85″. Courtesy the artist.

121. Peter Dean, *Evil Eye Drive In,* 1970. Oil on canvas, 10′ x 8′. Courtesy the artist.

who chooses to demystify existing American dreams. What greater myth exists than that of "sports in America"? Here, in Rosofsky's painting, we see the idiocy of the *Baseball Player* (*Ill. 123*). The romance of the sport is somewhat diminished by Casey, who sits dwarfed and surrounded by elegance and baroque decoration, draped in opulent affluence, still caught in the action that brought him to this: catching the ball. In the painting *Homage* (*Ill. 124*), Rosofsky gives us his vision of the myth of beauty: "You, too can have beautiful eyes if you use. . . ." She stands, stunted, grotesque, and ugly, admiring her prime and proper stature; she smells good, tastes good, has kissing sweet breath. Thirteen billion dollars were spent last year for cosmetics.

Absurd Humanism gives the viewer up-

122. Joseph Hirsch, *Al Dente*, 1966. Oil on canvas, 16″ x 12″. Courtesy Forum Gallery, Inc., New York.

123. Seymour Rosofsky, *Baseball Player*, 1966. Oil on canvas, 45″ x 35″. Courtesy the artist.

124. Seymour Rosofsky, *Homage,* 1965. Oil on canvas, 63½″ x 49″. Courtesy the artist.

125. Philip Sherrod, *The Buitoni Goddess,* 1970. Oil on canvas, 42″ x 44″. Courtesy the artist.

setting fantasies, demonstrating that the imagination can think up nothing as upsetting as reality itself. We live in a world where destruction is rationalized as necessary behavior, where goodness is synonymous with winning, where the subways of New York are acceptable, broadcast television desirable, and war admirable. A world of libido out of control could not be considered any more harmful to human well-being than a world of oppression and repression. Philip Sherrod and S. Clay Wilson, one a painter and the other a cartoonist, both bombard the viewer with fantasies of contempt for the death-promoting environment. Their images are mindscapes of people living the paranoia of American authoritarianism. And, if these dreams are explosive or exaggerated, it is because real lives are so repressed, so vacuous, and so distant from human needs.

In Sherrod's absurdist works, the writhing contours of his images, the semen orgy of sexual excess, the passion colors, flow with the rhythms of the body, and the nerves of human energy (see III. 125). Sherrod and Wilson are contemptuous of the automatons that have inherited the earth; their art shocks us, and reminds us that it is still not too late to contact our humanity.

S. Clay Wilson creates the American nightmare. In *Victorious Captain Whipple*

126. S. Clay Wilson, *Victorious Captain Whipple and the Survivors of His Crew Gather About the Slain Giant—They'll Eat Hearty That Night,* 1967. Ink on paper, 7¼″ x 9½″. Courtesy the artist.

127. S. Clay Wilson, *You Don't Know and They Don't Know,* 1967. Ink on paper, 7¼″ x 9½″. Courtesy the artist.

128. Peter Saul, *Mr. Welfare,* 1969. Oil on canvas, 93″ x 120″. Courtesy Darathea Speyer, Paris.

. . . (*Ill. 126*), we see the penis, the force of sexual drive and pleasure, the hidden reality: the prick, that part of Gulliver the little men fear. Ripping, stabbing, and slashing, they partake in rituals of repression legitimized by laws against positions of sexual pleasure, against homosexuality, against public nudity, against fornication with birds (in the State of Washington), and which, in a larger context, leads to all of the castrations of modern life, among them racism and war. If modern man is to best serve as the functionary of the technological environment, it is his penis that must come off, and here, in this Wilson fantasy, off it comes.

In *You Don't Know and They Don't Know* (*Ill. 127*), the nightmare of castration becomes the terror of sexual extremism. This is the licentious orgy all America mortally fears—the "total degradation" of the species—though not nearly, even at its worst, more depraved than one B-52 bombing run. This is the vision of the worst of it—the doom of America, the absence of all morality and order—thrust upon us by the young, the hippies, the LSD crazies, and the freaks. Ruination? Or, given the nature of actions we find acceptable, maybe just another serious exploration of the new morality with which to hawk *Time* magazine.

If Wilson maps the topology of the nightmare America dreads, artist Peter Saul maps the geography of the "American Reality." Everything eventually gets incorporated into a Saul work: the corporate state, the oppression of the blacks, the programming of children (*see Ill. 128*), ideological propaganda, and even the artist himself and the very gallery system through which he sells his art (*see Ill. 129*). His is an encompassing satire on the mechanics of this world. He demystifies language and intellectuality, because he despises what conceals from us what our world actually amounts to. Some will argue that his vision of poverty and affluence, of capital gain and human loss, is too simplified, that a more complex analysis is required. Sure.

The crucifixion of Donald Duck on Saul's frequently repeated cross, the incarnation of Ken Kesey's "Big Nurse," the fantasy of the Cold War, the war on poverty, the Commie pervert, Vietnamization, and the "rational" leader, are some of the victims of Saul's visual wit. For Saul, absurdity is environmental. Some may feel that his dayglo parody of Nixon's sexuality is offensive (*see Ill. 130*). Saul would argue, I suppose, that extremism in the images of art is no vice.

Saul Steinberg is another absurdist whose vision is environmental. He is the visual lexicographer of absurd terrain. In *Il Gabinetto del Proprio Niente* (*Ill. 131*), Steinberg has created the environment of insanity and contradiction, possibility and demolition, irrationality and aspiration, time and homeostasis, life and death. Here are the bits of our world—the files, stairs, and charts to an irrational tomorrow. Steinberg's unique accomplishment is the comprehensible but mysterious topography of human environments that is the continuing achievement of his art.

In various ways, Clayton Bailey, Jim Nutt, Gladys Nilsson, and the Mexican Brian Nissen create absurd caricatures of our time. Bailey satirizes the corporation man, the general, the cop, and the power hungry. For Bailey, the tough guy, the Hell's Angel (*see Ill. 132*), is best understood when seen as a poor fool— domesticated, and placed as sculpture on the living room table. Nissen creates active and spontaneous visual metaphors for the chewers, the biters, the starched and self-satisfied individuals (*see Ill. 133*)

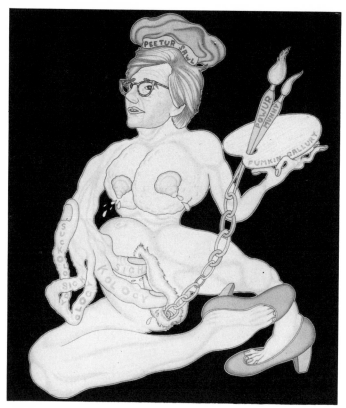

129. Peter Saul, *Self-Portrait,* 1971. Day-glo watercolor and colored pencil on illustration board, 41″ x 34″. Courtesy the artist.

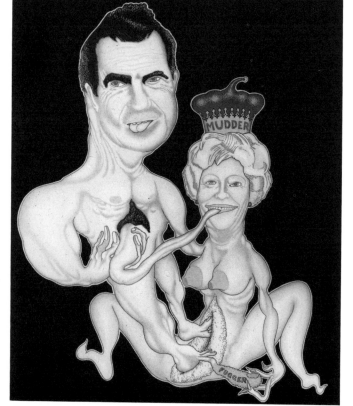

130. Peter Saul, *Nixon and Queen Mudder,* 1970. Gouache with pencil, 43½″ x 36″. Courtesy Allan Frumkin Gallery, New York.

131. Saul Steinberg, *Il Gabinetto del Proprio Niente,* 1966. Water-color, ink, and pastel, 29″ x 23″. Collection Adelaide de Menil, New York. Courtesy Sidney Janis Gallery, New York.

132. Clayton Bailey, *Hell's Angel Mask,* 1967. Latex rubber, life-size. Courtesy the artist.

133. Brian Nissen, *Injection,* 1970. Mixed media, approx. 20″ x 25½″. Courtesy the artist.

134. Gladys Nilsson, *Being Freatened,* 1969. Watercolor on paper, 18⅞″ x 10¾″. Courtesy the artist.

who exist in that daily state Gladys Nilsson portrays as *Being Freatened* (*Ill. 134*). Nutt's enigmatic imagery is filled with the bits and pieces of the absurdity of existence (*see Ill. 135*); without order, without logical connections, composed of fragments, the dim realizations, psychic thoughts, and emotional states are put together in a fashion that creates the experience of the confusion and morphology of the mind of modern man.

Best known of the new cartoonists is Robert Crumb, who can safely be considered the genius of the genre. Crumb's figures have entertained, informed, and humored one generation, and have been considered offensive and un-American by another. With a potent ability to identify a whole personality by exaggeration of one or two of its traits, Crumb's vision is populated by a world of people caught in vitiated metaphors of their own lives. Unwilling to debate with critics about the originality of his iconography, his formal organization, and his "careful" use of line to define the figure, Crumb places his visions in comic books, which can be had by all, and which, as can be seen in *Drawing Cartoons Is Fun!* (*Ill. 136*), show definite contempt for critical debate.

Crumb's "morbid" sense of humor is the alter ego to "normal behavior" (*see Ill. 137*). Do we not learn through television for example, to laugh at the pain of others, and to handle human difficulties with pistols and grenades?

In Crumb's view, we are all artists, insofar as we reveal awareness of ourselves, our potential, and our environment. Crumb demolishes the ideology of art: "After all, folks, it's only lines on paper." Art is no longer precious; it is an experience communicated in diverse ways, through personal vision, in all possible media, for as many to experience as possible. To the art world, Crumb's message might be that hell is paved with good connections; let your fingers do the walking.

By this time, Crumb is a tradition within the underground. His personal iconography, the "lighter-than-air boys," the stoned freaks, "The Crumps," "Mr. Natural," are instantly recognizable to an enormous number of older and younger viewers, who have dribbled with laughter at his depiction of American pathology.

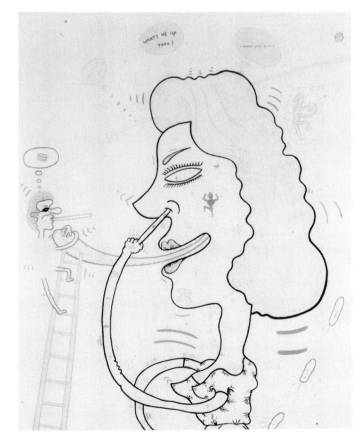

135. Jim Nutt, *Little Laddy Lady Ladder Climber,* 1967. Acrylic on Plexiglas, 36" x 30". Collection Peter Saul.

136. Robert Crumb, *Drawing Cartoons is Fun!*, 1969. Ink on paper, 9¾" x 6½". Courtesy the artist.

137. Robert Crumb, *Morbid Sense of Humor,* 1969. Ink on paper,
9¾″ x 6½″. Courtesy the artist.

Some think that Crumb's kind of humor is disgusting. Sure. But in contrast to the programmed and packaged images of America, the behaviors that are justified by salaries only, the consumerism that is the staple diet of society, and the neglect of human needs, the vision of Crumb, and other cartoonists, is the first effective alternative channel for a countercultural experience in the visual arts; somewhat analogous, I would add, to the subversive nature of many rock lyrics.

Of course, the new cartoonists would have had more difficulty, were it not for the genius of Jules Feiffer. Feiffer was really the first to bring comic strip characters to the underground. If Bernard seems slightly less maladjusted these days, if Feiffer's *Dance to Spring* creates nostalgia, and if the *Village Voice* seems less than a tenuous publication, these diminish little the ongoing wit, talent, and abrasive morality found in Feiffer's absurdist Humanist art.

Critics who have a need to distinguish high art from low have been reluctant to confer status to the comic book, though they have had less difficulty finding aesthetic justifications for action painting, earth art, and conceptual art. In fact, a common rationalization for the rejection of Humanist art takes the form of the assertion that the art is not art at all. Daumier's cartoons, once rejected, are now esteemed. Goya, considered in his own time as a portrait painter, was thought to have abandoned his true art to satisfy an obsession with etchings. Philip Evergood's paintings, once the object of scorn, are now prized. The ethnic images of artists like Jacob Lawrence, long considered to be mere "folk art," and not "real" art, are now found in most museum collections. Temporal distance, and the ability to sterilize nonestablishment art, seem to be the basic criteria for judging when it is time to accept a work as art. Slowly, Robert Crumb's cartoons are beginning to make their way into museum shows.

The absurdists are least appreciated by critics who are deeply disturbed by what they consider to be the offensive qualities of their images. One of the best of the absurdists, Philip Sherrod, had a show reviewed in the February 13, 1971 issue of the *New York Times*. The review was written by David L. Shirey:

In the catalogue to this show there is a photograph of Mr. Sherrod in which he has bent his head and seems to be covering his eyes. I assume that he has just looked at his paintings and can't believe he has created such a mess. The subject is mankind, his fall from grace into such sins as greed and lust, especially lust. There is no redemption for Mr. Sherrod's sinners. But then there is no redemption for his canvases. There is no technique, no style, no perception or vision. There is nothing.[57]

How do we account for this irresponsible journalism? The critic was obviously upset by Sherrod's paintings, because he states, "There is no technique." But Sherrod has an individual and highly sophisticated technique, based on the rhythms of his painting, his color, his sheer volume of paint, and his display of energy. Though his paintings sometimes might look superficially derivative of Van Gogh, they are individual, a result of the artist's ability to dissociate himself from himself, and enter into the psyche of those he chooses as models. Sherrod is able to take psychic voyages through the perceptions of others. His studio (*Color-plate V*), populated by a world of faces, minds, and bodies, is an environment—filled with all the sensations of humanity.

What repels critic Shirey, aside from his own rigidity, is that Sherrod's world of human fantasy and charades is an honest vision of what others see as the "proper" world and "proper" values. Sherrod's canvases (*see Ill. 138*) are peopled by figures masturbating and having lustful sex; they are parodies of the dead, sterile, archaic lives characterized by the job, the office, the corporation, the subway car, the cafeteria. These characters take time out from their antiseptic lives to give birth to impulse, force, and drive. For Sherrod, sensation is pure and real. Sherrod's allegiance is to the energy, the life—the motion—the pleasure of living. If his iconography is sometimes extreme, it is because our life situation is extreme. The impulse to pleasure, so remote from our castrated daily existences, keeps these beings alive.

He paints on the streets, and combines the faces found in the crowd with the fantasies of these people groping for life. The computer does not have illnesses, emptiness, neuroses; man does. Sherrod's fantasies are a reversal of normal

V. Philip Sherrod, studio photograph. Courtesy the artist.

VI. Melvin Zabarsky, *The Argentinian Cyclist,* 1969–70. Oil on canvas, 50″ x 54″. Courtesy the artist.

VII. Leon Golub, *Seated Boxer II,* 1960. Lacquer, 91″ x 86″. Courtesy the artist.

VIII. Maryan S. Maryan, Untitled, 1968. Oil on canvas, 30″ x 24″. Courtesy Galerie Claude Bernard, Paris.

existence, in the hope that the communal conversation is not over. Sherrod's vision is a vigorous assertion of individual man.

No vision? The form and content are meshed; the activity of the images and the rhythm of the painting are one. The critic speaks of the "fall from grace into such sins as greed and lust." Missing the ironic commentary on a species once capable of pleasure, and now fallen from grace into storage, the critic concludes that "there is nothing." If the critic is right, then the studio bursting with painted psychic lives is vacuous. If the critic is wrong, *he* is vacuous.

Absurd Humanism is, today, perhaps the most antagonistic Humanist art. It is damned for being too strong, and coopted if it is too mild. A case in point is Edward Paschke's *RFK at Arlington* (*Ill. 139*). Paschke's work is a satire of the American way of death, and of, specifically, how John F. Kennedy's death was translated into the hero myth. Robert Kennedy kneels at his brother's graveside. The

138. Philip Sherrod, *Mrs. Christ's Crucifixion,* 1970. Oil on canvas, 93″ x 78″. Courtesy the artist.

139. Edward Paschke, *RFK at Arlington,* 1970. Oil on canvas, 58″ x 72″. From *Each in His Own Way,* the Commemorative Art Collection of the Florists' Transworld Delivery Association. Courtesy Edward Gottlieb & Associates, Public Relations, New York, for Florists' Transworld Delivery.

painting is bathed in a candy-coated atmosphere, complete with red, white, and blue dayglo sky. Death is, in America, a ritual of eulogies, memorials, and souvenirs.

The subtlety of the work, and its understated satire, was utterly missed by the Florists' Transworld Delivery Association, who selected the work for their collection, and actually used it in their advertising. In their booklet explaining the *Each in His Own Way* collection, they state that *RFK at Arlington* . . . is doubly stirring in its appeal to sorrow and sympathy because we know—but none of the bystanders and mourners on that occasion did—that another tragedy is looming on the horizon."[58] It is not known if those who have seen the advertisement using Paschke's painting are as blind to its satirical intention as those who find sorrow in the work; either we are dealing here with an indication that absurdist art fails when it is not bold, or that Mr. Paschke has pulled the wool, not over his own eyes, but over those of his collectors. It is a case in point that demonstrates to what absurdity the uses of absurd Humanism can be put. Obviously not all absurdist works can be effective when "words cannot express the emptiness you feel."

Humanistic Portraiture

Some years ago, Clement Greenberg wrote that painters "can no longer handle portraits and figures with true feeling. Society does not," he argued, "circulate an adequate notion of human personality to which they can refer."[59] In recent years, many artists—many more than can be discussed here—have participated in a reconstruction of portraiture. Though Greenberg's insights articulate the difficulties of creating contemporary portraiture, it is not correct to say that these difficulties have not been overcome.

By definition, portraiture is motivated by Humanistic concerns. The artist's choice to make human beings his subject matter is indicative of an overriding interest in how man is living, not in those things he lives with. However portraiture is achieved, it comes as a result of the decision to keep alive the significance of individual and group lives.

Today's portraiture does require a more complex vision than was common years ago. The artist who merely realistically renders human beings falls within the category of portrait artists, who are many in number, but on the periphery of innovation. If portraiture is to prove exciting today, it must penetrate the matrix of the human psyche. We are not merely what we seem to be. Modern portraiture must take into account the environment, as well as the personality, the psyche, and the history of the subject, and communicate its understanding by characterization, expression, and atmosphere. Contemporary portraiture can be as varied as Melvin Zabarsky's narrated lives, Alice Neel's historical lives, or Philip Sherrod's sensuous hold on the energy and identity of his sitters. In all cases, portraiture differs from other forms of the Humanist intention because of the artist's willingness to suspend or relax judgment in favor of empathy for the subject.

Perhaps best known for the authenticity of their empathetic portraiture are Moses Soyer and Raphael Soyer. For decades, they have both created an honest, dignified portraiture, which has proved to be influential on many younger portraitists. Another portraitist of indirect but considerable influence is David Levine, who is well known for his perceptive, potent, and often hilariously drawn characterizations of political and literary celebrities. It is partly due to Levine's persistence as an ironic chronicler that, at this point in time, many have been reawakened to the insight and pleasure afforded by this genre. Contemporary portraiture is increasingly thought of as no longer a second rate form of creation, but a valid and important expression of Humanist intention.

Alice Neel is one of the most convincing portraitists. Her aim is to create a history of people. "For me," says Neel, "people are the first premise, and my work is a monument to them. . . . I believe in art as history."[60] Typical of Neel's creations is her portrait of Andy Warhol (*Ill. 140*). Here, the Humanist comes to look at the "what's happening" artist. This fleshy, rather sadly sagging, over-age, yet somehow juvenile, being sits quietly, bearing the scars of his survival. The painter feels no communication from her subject; Warhol's eyes are closed, his head is held stiffly, as if pained, and his arms enclose a listless body. Here is the image of Andy Warhol—the artist who redefined art as nondescript and non-unique—turned into a nondescript and less than unique creature; Neel shows us the artist made into the image of his art.

One major strength of contemporary

140. Alice Neel, *Andy Warhol,* 1970. Oil on canvas, 60″ x 40″. Courtesy the artist.

141. Charles White, *J'Accuse! No. 1,* 1966. Charcoal on paper, 50″ x 36″. Collection Dr. and Mrs. Bertram V. Karpf. Courtesy Heritage Gallery, California.

portraiture is its created images of social groups, and individuals within them, who have historically been excluded as subject matter for past portraiture. Several important artists have created portraits of the disenfranchised: blacks, Indians, and Mexican Americans.

Perhaps best known for his dedication to the communication of black experience and black perception is Charles White. In an environment that has spawned a virulent racism, White has steadfastly created images of black strength and endurance, black character, and forceful transcendence of the psychic and material oppressions of black people (*see Ill. 141*). What more can the black artist do? While the white critic may advise the black artist to be an "artist," to consider content a relatively minor question, in comparison with aesthetic ones, the major black artists, including Charles White, have committed themselves to the portrayal of their experience, and the depiction of the proud survival of the oppressed.

Another portraitist of his people is Eldzier Cortor. His *Study No. 34* (*Ill. 142*) is the embodiment of the inner and outer strengths of his subject. The figure consumes the canvas. The head is monumental; the strong, bold features imply excessive physical work. Yet the head communicates serenity, and makes this an image of dignity and beauty.

In *Pomo* (*Ill. 143*), Joseph Raffael has incarnated the strength of all Indian people in his portrait of one Indian. The intensity and directness of his gaze shows a man who has not been defeated by the degradation forced upon his life and his people. The details of the eyes, nose, and mouth of the Indian's rugged, weathered face indicate both the dignity of the individual, and the historical endurance of his people. Once powerful and self-possessed, now threatened by tuberculosis and poverty, the Indian is taken today to be the shaman of youth seeking a way out of a despiritualized and materialistic environment. But, whatever place he is assigned, this portrait demands that we confer on him his unique and vital identity.

Another approach to portraiture is pursued by Melvin Zabarsky, a creator of narrative paintings that derive their strength from literal interpretations of history. One of his most satisfying works, *The Argentinian Cyclist* (*Colorplate VI*), presents a multiple image perspective of the life of Che Guevara. Here is Guevara the cyclist; Guevara the medical student; Guevara the adventurer; Guevara the revolutionary; Guevara the myth. Though there have been many attempts to por-

tray Guevara, few show us more than one glimpse of the man they prefer to admire. Zabarsky attempts the whole, without losing the identity of the parts. Zabarsky has continued, for over a decade, to "paint large narrative pictures which should," he says, "say something about my being here in America"[61] (*see Ill. 144*).

Many artists involved in creating portraits of our time begin with the specifics of their own life, and later, as their art develops, generalize their experience into a universal one. As was discussed earlier, this is how the art of May Stevens progressed. *The Living Room,* an earlier work of portraiture, serves as the initial starting point for the more comprehensive art she develops later.

One of the better portrait painters is Philip Sherrod. His studio is the archetypal Humanist abode, filled with the in-

142. Eldzier Cortor, *Study No. 34,* 1971. Oil on canvas, 14" x 18". Courtesy the artist.

143. Joseph Raffael, *Pomo,* 1970. Oil on canvas, 79″ x 59½″. Collection University Art Museum, Berkeley, California.

there is not sufficient space to be able to discuss all the work that deserves attention. I have tried to suggest the importance of those artists who have had to be omitted, by their inclusion in the artists' reference section at the end of the book. All the portraitists found there have in common the insistence that they will not let life go by unnoticed, will not relegate human lives to obscurity because of the unfulfilling nature of contemporary experience. The Humanist portraitist feels obligated to respond to the human beings who comprise the lonely crowd, of which he is a part, and from which he is often estranged.

The Possibility of Transcendence

Throughout past chapters, we have seen Humanist artists who attempt to comprehend, re-create, communicate about, and respond to our crisis and our diminished

escapable vibrations of the personalities and character of those he paints. In *The Holy Dumbbell* (*Ill. 145*), the artist turns his vision upon himself. Here is Sherrod, his head turned sideways, listening but suspicious. The body is well-developed, and suggestive of the force, power, and muscle of the painter. The eye is intent; the canvas is filled with spirits, emotions, and things unseen and unsaid. The artist's mouth is shut, perhaps stilled by what he thinks he knows. And, as the eye moves over the canvas, and becomes preoccupied by its nuances and subtleties, the force of the work, and the dynamics of the paint, begin to suggest that the artist is himself awed by the insight of the brush.

There are a number of other exciting Humanist portraitists, but, unfortunately,

144. Melvin Zabarsky, *Krupp and the Egyptian Belly Dancer,* 1969. Oil on canvas, 44″ x 36″. Courtesy the artist.

145. Philip Sherrod, *The Holy Dumbbell,* 1970. Oil on canvas, 56" x 50". Courtesy the artist.

lives. Their experiences are motivated partly by an overwhelming feeling of discontent, and partly in the hope that we are still able to redirect our energies toward a new environment that offers greater humanity than the present one.

The expression of discontent, however, comes easier than optimism. The Humanist is on the defensive. The artist is surrounded by a world of unreal images, of believed lies, and by a complacent humanity. Despite his holistic aspiration, the Humanist has been forced to concern himself primarily with those aspects of contemporary experience that communicate the failure of modern life to satisfy human life. Though the Humanist wants to integrate all the faculties of man, he is required to maintain steadfastly his position of cultural criticism, believing that only a rigorous countercultural art will fill the void of conscience and concern prevalent in the arts today. Thus, he has

chosen to create what other artists ignore, and what critics and art historians insist must not be created. Clearly, the opportunities for positive statements are few.

How does the Humanist offer, if not optimism, at least some elements of a hopeful vision of man? How does one create the experience of human worth, of genuine possibility, without slipping back into an outworn romanticism? These questions touch upon the major task of Humanist art today: the creation of an art that communicates both death and life.

To be able to transcend the present situation, the artist must first overcome his own alienation. I have preferred to focus on two artists who have created the possibility of transcendence. Since the ways they have accomplished this feat are very different, I have thought it would be particularly worthwhile to con-

146. Leon Golub, *Fallen Fighter*, 1971. Acrylic, 9'8" x 9'2". Courtesy the artist.

sider them in isolation from the rest. I am speaking of Leon Golub and Maryan S. Maryan. Golub has secured a balanced vision of man's actuality and his possibility by creating monumental images, appropriate totems for contemporary man. Maryan has succeeded with an art that develops through a linear serial format extending over most of his creative life. Both artists have been able to find a personal vision that incorporates both the present crisis and the Utopian potential of man. They have created the fusion of art, life, and man. In this time of fragmentation, they have developed an integrative art suggestive of the totality of experience. These transcendental Humanists have seen beyond the apocalypse. Theirs is the most holistic art to be found within the Humanist intention.

Over the past two decades, Leon Golub has planted the seed, nurtured, nourished, and developed a race of giant men, who are now given to us on very large canvases. The fetal mutants that characterized his earlier work were stumpy, splatted, malformed little humans. They have grown and developed over the years, and now exist as monumental figures (see III. 146). But grandiose images would suggest man as hero, man as fulfilled prince of his potential. Man is not that big—not that potent—so Golub assaults the painting, lays bare the giants to erosion and decay, and attacks the totems with human actuality. Thus, his figures are either burnt out or stripped down in an aggressive act that is one of the most unique manifestations of reduction in modern art. Poised on unstretched canvas, the figures are primitive and unadorned; they are robbed of flesh and fullness. Thus, man has enormous stature, while, at the same time, he is vulnerable, laid bare, disastrously subject to time and history. The images are strong, structured, and muscular, but they are also tender, bloodied, sheared, and tormented by skin that no longer protects, no longer regenerates. Though alive and functioning, they are still malformed, with muscles, tendons, and nerves exposed to the corrosive atmosphere of our time (*Colorplate VII*).

In an age of spiritual dissolution, Golub has created totemic myths. The literal figures are great in their size, and retarded in their ability to survive. Golub has given man his destructive power, and denied him what he needs to be able to endure. We see them as power without flesh, strength without emotion, violence without reason. The gargantuan is a pathological victim: man without his humanity. Thus, man is synthesized into one vision: god, and a "useless passion." Golub has created the epic view of the twentieth century: The dream of universal power and self-possessed stature, the nightmare of the use of power, and the failure to secure well-being are brought together in totemic images of our plight and our hope.

Golub's art—from his earlier, less ambitious human fetal imprints, to the burnt out men like *Horseman II* (*III. 147*), to the giant in *Gigantomachy III* (*III. 148*)—constitutes the development of a modern purgatory. Man exists in a half-life, facing the next century with immense power, and with, perhaps, fatal susceptibility. Like the dinosaurs that once claimed the earth was theirs, mankind is revealed in Golub's work as a group of admirable creatures lacking what is needed for completion and survival. His work is a monumental question of destiny, in terms that demand we supply an answer. Are we to be the dead colossus, or can we turn our powers toward our own well-being?

Leon Golub has created one of the most ambitious representational arts in our time, identifiable by the large size of his figures. Maryan S. Maryan has also created one of the most ambitious representational arts of our time, identifiable by the small and out-of-fashion size of his canvases.

When he was twelve years old, he was interred in a concentration camp, where he spent the next six years of his life. Left for dead several times, Maryan learned first hand of the macabre innovations of the twentieth century. Maryan has survived the hell of that time, with its authorities, its brutal "rationality," its death pile, and its unending march of murder-

ers. He has few of our illusions. He has seen the bottom of man's pit of inhumanity; whatever he has come to believe has not been quickly acquired.

About twenty-five years ago, Maryan began to piece his life together. Freed of the camp, facing open land for the first time in six years, perhaps tortured by the death cries and agonized images of camp victims, this self-taught painter began a battle with the images of death and the memories of the dying. Pitting his sanity against the steeled vision of bloodsoaked images and tormented humanity forever etched in his mind, he began to attack

147. Leon Golub, *Horseman II,* 1960. Lacquer, 81" x 93". Collection Mr. and Mrs. Gene R. Summers, Illinois.

148. Leon Golub, *Gigantomachy III,* 1966. Acrylic, 9½′ x 18′. Courtesy the artist.

149. Maryan S. Maryan, Untitled, 1962. Oil on canvas, 50″ x 50″. Courtesy the artist.

150. Maryan S. Maryan, Untitled (personage with feet in air), 1964. Oil on canvas, 40" x 40". Courtesy Allan Frumkin Gallery, New York.

those responsible for the butchery. His art became an exorcism of authority, a psychological journey into and beyond the crisis of contemporary life. Today, his art is not about freedom and despair; it is liberation itself. He challenges the images of his keepers with paint-laden brush, creating and re-creating them in a progression leading to his transcendence.

First, we see them as authorities: ordered, precise, intense (*see III. 149*). In each progressive painting, we see power ridiculed by gestures of infantilism, sickness, foolishness, absurdity, and pathological collapse (*see III. 150*). As time goes on, Maryan becomes more aggressive in his attack. Now these representational images are transformed into guts and bowels, blood vessels and nerve endings. No longer ridiculed, we now see them choked on their own organs, suffocating on innards that come out of their mouths (*Colorplate VIII*). The bodies are painted with colors of organs, blood, muscle fiber, and cortex of brain. Maryan is moving all the time to the destruction of those who had wished to destroy him.

He finally dismembers the violators of humanity. Now dissected, torn, unrecognizable, they exist as impoverished abstractions, without faces, with profusion of color and death chant. Maryan has destroyed the assassins of Marat. Purged from his psyche is the vulgar, foul memory of the worst of our time.

It is an odyssey that does not end with the present. From the degraded hovels of the concentration camp, to the destruction of the images of authority, the artist struggles to find belief. Now Maryan creates images of new life in the heartland of the technological machine. The new canvases are filled by images of rebirth: of children's bodies inhabited by old and aged faces, each face identified by some first gesture of childhood. Through this serial painting process, through art, and through cultural testimony, a human being has regained his sense of the possible. It is one of the most convincing demonstrations of transcendence to be found in modern art. Out of the holocaust, Maryan has come to believe again in man. This is Humanism in art.

THE FUTURE OF HUMANIST ART

Visual arts do not relate to mass audiences. Visual objects are pictures on the wall, and sculptures on the floor. They offer an involvement that is more personal and less communal. Though there have been numerous attempts to create alternative gallery structures, they usually have not been successful. This is due to a number of factors, each of which is significant. The visual artist is a loner; his art is almost always made in solitude. He exists within an environment that is highly competitive, severely limiting, and without collective structures. Thus, he must deal with the environment by himself. Alone, he will never be able to create viable alternatives to the existing gallery structures, the museum show, and the art magazine. Further, because, unlike performing artists, he creates an object, he can be separated from the thing he creates. It can be marketed, exhibited, and distributed without him. He is necessary only for its creation. Because his creation can be so treated, the visual arts have remained structurally rooted to institutional frameworks.

The dilemma of the Humanist artist today is, in part, the dilemma of all artists. As long as the Humanist artist, working in isolation, remains totally dependent on institutional structures, he will be victimized by the prevailing value system. Because the manner in which art is currently exhibited does much to undermine the potency of Humanist art, because patronage generally does not support what is critical of patrons, and because Humanist art is subject to the judgment of "poor taste," it will remain primarily an "underground," a less visible inten-

tion, in art, and will only emerge strongly when new formats are developed for the exhibition, sale, and collection of Humanist works.

The Humanist artist is in a bind. Because he is still working within the tradition of the unique art object, he remains dependent on the only system we have for the exhibition and collection of these objects. And, because he is an artist, he will be reluctant to exert energies in the direction of creating viable alternatives, because such energies take him from his art. Finally, it is by no means certain that efforts to create alternatives to the marketing, distribution, and exhibition of Humanist art can succeed within the larger organization of the cultural environment.

In the absence of supportive alternatives to the existing structures within the cultural environment, Humanist artists have developed several interesting responses to their situation. Many of the artists in this book, while relatively obscure in America, have received wide recognition in Europe. Artists as diverse in their styles as Leon Golub, Peter Saul, and Seymour Rosofsky, for example, have received shows, critical acclaim, and support within the European cultural environment. Outside of the United States, they have not been considered eccentric, outdated, or "literary"; they have, instead, been seen as important artists working in an international style. It is to be remembered that American films were first treated seriously by Europeans. One may say the same of contemporary American image makers. European attitudes have not been based on how well artists have fit into New York-centered hierarchical structures. With some degree of detachment, Europeans have been able to make judgments without panic.

In fact, one of the biases against Humanist art is a reaction to the art's international orientation. Since Abstract Expressionism turned New York, and by implication the United States, into the "art center of the world," there has been a steadfast attempt to maintain American leadership in art. Working out of a curiously old-fashioned imperialist logic, many have felt that the art that must be supported is the art that is explicitly American: the art that maintains American cultural prominence. Humanism is a tradition in art that is not solely American, and, because it does not pretend to support an ideology of invention, it is thought by some to be "un-American," in the sense that, if it were to become generally acceptable, it would endanger the privileged position of American art. "I like your work very much," one gallery owner told Philip Sherrod, "but I can't show it. It is too European."[62] Europeans are not burdened with the idea of American art, and have been far more appreciative of many American Humanists than have the Humanists' own countrymen.

In their attempt to overcome the difficulty of exhibiting Humanist works, artists have often chosen to create murals in public spaces. Not only can the works be seen by large numbers of people, but the scale of most mural spaces is particularly suited to Humanist intentions and figurative imagery. Since the most outstanding Humanist in our century, José Orozco, was a muralist, there are historical precedents motivating Humanists to turn to murals.

Recently, there has been a resurgence of interest in murals—what some have heralded as a Renaissance in muralism. The revival of muralism has not come about because of any change in the pattern of funding; it is as difficult to find mural commissions today as it ever was. The Renaissance in murals is coincidental with greater community control over the institutions and spaces within a community. Because community groups are more receptive to common unifying experiences, and because they are searching for a community identity, they have been much more supportive of artist projects than have the politicians and bureaucrats previously in control. Much important public art created in recent years has been without commission, and achieved only because artist and community were able to get together.

The collaboration of artist and community in mural projects is not a theoretical question. In 1967, the *Wall of Respect,* a truly impressive mural, was completed. It has been painted on a burnt-out shell in Chicago. Since that time, there have been sixty murals painted in Chicago alone, and untold numbers in cities across this country.

Photographs of the murals, which unfortunately cannot be shown here, tell the story of artist-resident collaboration. Missing is the usual apparatus: museum, gallery, dealer, critic, and art magazine article—the middlemen who intercede between artist and public. But missing here is also the story of artists like Bill Walker, Mark Rogovin, John Weber, and Eugene Eda—artists who have explored and achieved a new working relationship between their creative expression and the new "patrons," people who have elected to interact and live with art as a vital part of their experience. I wish there were enough space to tell the story of Walker's *The Wall of Understanding,* or of Rogovin's innumerable interactions with the community as he worked on *Free Angela Davis, Free All Political Prison-*

ers, or of Venita Green's feelings when her mural depicting the lives of black women was defaced with white paint, and turned into a still greater symbol of black experience marred by white domination. The muralist movement is the experience of artist and community, of social consciousness and emotional interaction, of life experience and artistic experience. It is an event that must be participated in; it is a story that must be told someday soon.

Humanists have also turned to the cartoon, the magazine, and the comic book as avenues for mass exposure to their work. The drawings of Emory in the Black Panther magazine, the comic books of Crumb, Spain, and S. Clay Wilson, and the magazine drawings of Levine and Steinberg all demonstrate the viability of these alternatives to the cultural apparatus.

Still another development is the widespread availability of poster art. Posters of protest have served as a major graphic expression of the peace movement, radicalism, and Humanist art. The political posters of Tomi Ungerer; the burning satirical posters of Ron Cobb; and the many posters evolved by collectives of artists flooding underground, and occasionally overground, America with a steady stream of Humanist art for their walls, all demonstrate the viability of these approaches to the creation of Humanist art. The poster, though still considered a bastard child of the arts, will increasingly assume a more central position within the purview of Humanist creation.

Still another development, and perhaps the most significant one, is that many Humanist artists have come to the conclusion that they will only be effective by giving up the object entirely. Believing that, as long as they produce objects,

they are dependent on the existing cultural apparatus, and recognizing that the new consciousness is more concerned with events than with "things," these artists have become actional Humanists. Though I have specifically limited the range of this book to object creators, I do want to suggest the more lengthy discussion the actional Humanist deserves. The works of Tosun Bayrak and the activities of Jean Toche and Jon Hendricks of the Guerrilla Art action group are but two examples of many important innovations leading toward an actional Humanism.

In this connection, I think it is important to mention the work of Boris Lurie, whose "no" paintings, assemblages, and "altered men" series (see Ill. 151) show the destruction of the image, and the artist's refusal to comply with society's definition of his role as artist. The March Gallery scene in the early part of the 1960's, of which Boris Lurie and the late Sam Goodman were a part, can be thought of as the last aspect of object creation before actional Humanism.

The realization of actional Humanism is not to be confused with a happening. For one thing, a happening is usually a spontaneous visual-theatrical event; it is a type of artistic activity. The actional Humanist is concerned with changing life, not adding to the varieties of art. His efforts are directed toward an action, that, if successful, will artistically induce social change. The works of Bayrak, Toche, and Hendricks are representative of actional Humanism; their wish is to have impact on society through artistic expression—not to create a mass-participation artistic activity.

Though Tosun Bayrak's Death of a Car (Ill. 152) may still fall into the category of an object, it is experienced as an actual actional event. Death of a Car is not an image. It is a real car, with real entrails spilling out of it. It has no illusionary elements. The guts, skin, and blood are real. The distance between art and life is now infinitesimal. Bayrak's *Slaughter of the Lamb* and *Death of a Car,* raise the major questions pertaining to actional Humanism. Although Bayrak has freed himself from the gallery and the museum and has, in fact, developed an art with a mass audience, he may have also lost something in the process. His experience is so direct, so inseparable from life itself, that many among his audience are unable to elevate his experiences to a metaphorical symbolic level. Thus, while

Slaughter of a Lamb is the artist's symbolic expression of total disgust at the contemporary slaughter of all life, including human life, which we accept as reality, the actual slaughter of the lamb—the artist with axe in hand slashing at the animal—is itself so revolting to some that they feel that the artist has joined forces with the very evil he wishes to exorcise. It is felt by many that *Death of a Car* allows no reflection and thus no judgment, that it is too repulsive to serve as an object of insight. Yet, despite these concerns, which may in a few years be seen as conservative responses, there is a growing audience for this kind of work,

151. Boris Lurie, *Man, Altered,* 1964. Oil on canvas, 30″ x 20″. Courtesy the artist.

152. Tosun Bayrak, *Death of a Car,* 1968. Crushed car, entrails, and blood, life-size. Courtesy the
artist.

and a growing acceptance among that audience that this is what must be done if America is to see itself.

Jon Hendricks and Jean Toche are pioneers of actional Humanism. They have made at least one substantial discovery, and, although it will not be mentioned in art history books, it is one of the most impressive insights in contemporary art. Toche and Hendricks discovered, or, perhaps, rediscovered, that political action that would never be permitted or condoned is allowed, and often praised, if it is presented as art within the cultural context. Their tactics of disruption and confrontation, when practiced against such institutions as the Museum of Mod-

ern Art and the Metropolitan Museum of Art, have not been greeted with police clubs, jail sentences, and construction workers. For politics, when presented as art, is effective politics. When Toche, Hendricks, and Faith Ringgold arranged an event outside the cultural domain, specifically, when they set up the *People's Flag Show* at the Judson Memorial Church in New York City, they were arrested and prosecuted for desecration of the flag. A fitting metaphor for the despiritualization of man: What would have been tolerated and defensible as an exhibition at the Museum of Modern Art was, in a church, subject to police tactics, prosecution, and repression. As soon as

Toche and Hendricks presented themselves as organizers who have an interest in art, rather than as artists who sometimes organize, they were seen as political activists, not cultural ones.

Toche and Hendricks have paved the way for actional Humanism. They have been able to stimulate institutional change, bring attention to certain important issues, and create what are now classical patterns in actional events. It can be expected that greater numbers of Humanist artists will abandon the object, relate directly to mass audiences, and create political events that will be treated as cultural ones.

Actional Humanism brings into focus the relationships between art and culture and between culture and life. Humanism in art wants to influence human perceptions—a wish that is motivated by a desire to see changed life and changed lives. The Humanists desire impact, at a time when artists, at best, are permitted to be "news." Within the structural design of patronage, institutional values, and an art world that celebrates its libertarian attitudes, while rigidly perpetuating the *status quo,* the Humanist wants art to participate in the movement toward social change. He knows that art alone can change very little, but he also knows that, with change, there must be an art that supports change.

The Humanist sees the present course of Western society, maybe of all society, as a suicide trip. He does not wish to see more war, more pollution in the natural and human environments, and more values generating the worst in man. While our products self-destruct, the Humanist wants us to be aware that, among the mechanisms and the techniques, we have forgotten the requirements of human need. He asks that we open ourselves to a difficult art and see what we have become. Humanism is a jam in the programing. It creates those images and allegories that identify our task.

No art can change the cultural conditioning within the environment. No art can ensure that the voices of alarm will be heard. No art can sensitize a humanity that regards individual conscience as an unnecessary burden. But, despite the narrow interests of present patronage, despite the collective machinations of the cultural apparatus, despite the manipulation of art itself, there are many countercultural forces at work today. Humanism is one of them, and, if I have given it more exposure than it has previously received, and if I have articulated some of the reasons for its creation, I can end happily.

BRIEF BIOGRAPHIES
OF ARTISTS

Sometimes authors are required to resemble politicians; they, too, must work within the limits of the possible. Throughout this project, I maintained what proved to be an unrealistic approximation of the number of art works that could be discussed and reproduced. As the book moved from conception to publication, both words and photographs of works had to be deleted for reasons of space. In the end, I realized that no one book could give attention to the many deserving artists whose work I encountered. I have chosen here to give a biographical accounting of all the artists originally intended for inclusion. Although I regret that some could not appear in the text or among the illustrated works, I hope they will be seen as vital contributors to the development of Humanism in modern art.

· · ·

SIGMUND ABELES, Professor of Art at the University of New Hampshire, was born in New York in 1934. In 1969, Aquarius Press published a suite of his etchings, *Toward the End.* Abeles's work is represented in the collections of Bowdoin College, the Jewitt Art Center, the DeCordova Art Museum, and the Columbia Museum. "Etchings of Sigmund Abeles" was published in *American Artists* magazine, September, 1964.

BENNY ANDREWS was born in Georgia in 1930. He is a cochairman of the Black Emergency Cultural Coalition, an organization aimed at gaining greater representation for black artists. "The B.E.C.C.," an article written by Andrews, appeared in the Summer, 1970, issue of *Arts* magazine. In 1972, the A.C.A. Galleries, which represents his work, gave Andrews a one-man show, which included his latest work, *Trash.* The catalogue of this exhibition tells a great deal about this artist's work. Andrews currently lives in New York.

EDUARDO ARROYO was born in 1937 in Madrid. The work of this political Humanist has been exhibited in all the major cities of Europe. In 1970, his work was included in *"Kunst und Politik,"* an exhibition presented in Karlsruhe, Frankfurt, Wuppertal, and Basel. Arroyo currently lives in Milan and Rome.

MANUEL AYASO who was born in La Coruña, Spain, in 1934, moved to the United States in 1947. He now resides in Newark, New Jersey. His work is currently represented by the Forum Gallery in New York and can be found in the collections of the Whitney Museum of American Art, the Pennsylvania Academy of Fine Arts, the Butler Institute of American Art, and the New Jersey State Museum. John Canaday reviewed his work in two articles in the *New York Times* on December 8, 1968, and January 4, 1969.

FRANCIS BACON was born in Dublin in 1909. He now lives in London. He has had one-man exhibitions in all the major museums in Europe and the United States. Bacon's intention is to try "to paint the track left by human beings—like the slime left by snails." He is represented by Marlborough Fine Art Ltd. in London, which, in 1968, published *Francis Bacon: Recent Paintings,* a comprehensive catalogue of his latest work.

CLAYTON BAILEY, born in 1939 and now living in California, has created a menagerie of fanciful ceramic creatures of satiric intent. "I like my masks and critters," he has written. "I like the smell they make; their mess; them organic pores and blemishes of clay, skin-like rubber. I get to love them because they're ugly. They don't threaten me." His work is currently represented by the Lee Nordness Gallery in New York.

ENRICO BAJ was born in 1924 in Milan. His fanciful canvases, which mock the world of serious and powerful men, have been exhibited throughout Europe. The exhibition catalogue from the Chicago Museum of Contemporary Art, published in 1971, is an excellent reference to Baj's work. In the United States, his work is represented by Le Chat Bernard in Chicago.

RUDOLF BARANIK wants to create as a metaphor of contemporary existence "an absolute silence, but on the verge of turbulence . . . an arrested order, but tense and precarious, almost falling apart." Born in 1920 in Lithuania, he now resides in New York. His work is represented in the collections of the Moderna Museet in Stockholm, the Whitney Museum of American Art, the Museum of Modern Art, and the New York University and University of Massachusetts art collections.

LEONARD BASKIN, born in 1922 in Massachusetts, has had extensive one-man shows, and he is now represented by the Kennedy Galleries in New York. In 1952, Baskin founded the Gehenna Press, known as one of the outstanding presses in the United States. Baskin's sculpture, graphics, book design, and illustration depict "injured and brutalized man, alone, naked, and defenseless. My hero," Baskin states, "stands stoopingly up-right, pot-bellied and tight-assed, top heavy on his thin legs. He is spent and bewildered, frail and human. . . . And yet," Baskin says, "I hold man as collectively redemptible."

TOSUN BAYRAK, who was born in Istanbul in 1926, has studied in Istanbul, London, Paris, and California. His works, which include sculptures made of animal organs, and his events, which sometimes include the sacrifice of animals, and the anointment of persons with blood, have created controversy among artists in New York, where Bayrak lives. Bayrak's work can be found in the collections of the Guggenheim Museum, the Rose Art Museum, the Newark Museum, and the Trenton State Museum.

ROMARE BEARDEN was born in 1914 in Charlotte, North Carolina. In his work, Bearden explores "the particulars of the life I know best, those things common to all cultures." Represented by Cordier-Ekstrom Gallery in New York, Bearden was given a one-man exhibition at the Museum of Modern Art in 1971. Bearden also deserves recognition for his tireless efforts to bring talented and overlooked black artists to the public's attention. The exhibition catalogue from the Museum of Modern Art is an excellent source for further reference.

MIRIAM BEERMAN was born in 1923 in Rhode Island. She currently resides in Brooklyn. In 1971, Beerman was given a one-woman exhibition at the Brooklyn Museum. Beerman perceives her work "as a kind of biography and autobiography combined. The former relating to parts of the world at large. The latter, of course, a story of myself." In 1972, *The Enduring Beast,* a book edited and illustrated by Beerman, was published by Doubleday & Company. Beerman's work is represented by Graham Gallery in New York.

ARNOLD BELKIN was born in Canada in 1930. He lived in Mexico from 1948 to 1968, and since then has lived in New York. In 1972, Belkin exhibited his series on Marat at the Lerner-Heller Gallery in New York, which currently represents his work. The Marat paintings illustrate Belkin's concern "to express the human condition, above all man's inherent heroism in spite of the anxieties, fears and guilt feelings which assail him."

YEHUDA BEN-YEHUDA's kinetic sculptures of the victims of the holocaust have been exhibited throughout Europe, including one-man shows held at the Jerusalem, Haifa, and Tel Aviv Museums of Art, the Galleria Numero in Florence, and the New Vision Center in London. Born in Baghdad in 1933, Ben-Yehuda has made his home in New York and Tel Aviv since 1965. His work is represented by O. K. Harris Works of Art in New York.

ALAN BERMOWITZ was born in Brooklyn in 1939. He now lives in New York.

Bermowitz has been actively involved in the movement to create alternative structures to galleries and museums. On the board of "Museum," an artists' cooperative project, he assisted in the creation of a new environment, where artists worked, exchanged information, and exhibited. Bermowitz also creates light sculptures, which have been given two shows at O. K. Harris Works of Art in New York.

EDWARD BIBERMAN, an artist whose work has been exhibited throughout the United States says, "The closer we seemed to be coming to world catastrophe, the more urgent . . . the need to sing the praises of the planet we were close to destroying." Two books containing Biberman's work have been published— *Time and Circumstance* in 1968, and *The Best Untold* in 1954. Biberman was born in 1904 in Philadelphia, and presently lives in Los Angeles.

MICHAEL BIDDLE, son of the late George Biddle, is a printmaker whose works have been commissioned by the Associated American Artists Gallery in New York and by Artists Originals. Biddle was born in 1934 in New York. He has had several one-man shows, and his work is represented in the collections of the Metropolitan Museum of Art, the Albertine Graphische Sammlung in Vienna, the University of Minnesota, and Upsala College.

STANLEY BLEIFIELD, a sculptor, born in Brooklyn in 1924, now resides in Connecticut. He has had one-man shows at the i.f.a. gallery in Washington, D.C., and at the FAR Gallery in New York, both of which represent his work.

HYMAN BLOOM was born in Lithuania in 1913. He came to the United States in 1920, and he now lives in Brookline, Massachusetts. He is represented by the Terry Dintenfass Gallery in New York. Many of Bloom's drawings are reproduced in the exhibition catalogue, *The Drawings of Hyman Bloom,* published by the University of Connecticut Museum of Art in 1968. Among the collections in which his work is found are the Harvard

University art collection, the Whitney Museum of American Art, the Addison Gallery in Andover, the Museum of Modern Art, and the Smith College art collection.

RALPH BORGE was born in 1922 in Oakland, California. Borge is currently Professor of Art at the California College of Arts and Crafts. His work has been exhibited at the Banger Gallery in New York, and it is represented by the Gumps Gallery in San Francisco. In his untitled paintings, Borge attempts "to bring together symbols of some facets of the social milieu in which I have grown and present them in a mystical light."

KEN BOWMAN, born in 1937, now lives and works in New York. Bowman's work is represented by the Tibor de Nagy Gallery in New York, which gave him his most recent one-man show in 1972. Bowman's art, often based on old photographs taken in America in the early part of this century, are in the collections of the Utah Museum of Art, the University Art Museum in Berkeley, and the Salt Lake City Museum.

CHARLES BRAGG was born in Saint Louis in 1931. Bragg's work is in the permanent collections of the Dayton Art Museum, the Downey Museum of Art, the Wichita Art Museum, and the Long Beach Museum of Art. Bragg now lives in Woodlawn Hills, California. His work is represented by A.C.A. Galleries in New York.

JOHN BRATBY was born in 1928 in Wimbledon, England. Bratby expresses his Humanist orientation as follows: "I believe in painting that is by a human being, directly painted by him, by an individual. Painting that is about the human condition and his environment, and that in some way rejoices in this life we have." Many of Bratby's paintings are reproduced in *John Bratby,* a good reference book, published in 1961 by Studio Books, London.

GABRIELLE BRILL is a German-born artist who now resides in Hollywood, California. Images of the embryo are the recurrent subject matter in her work. In her etchings, collages, and drawings, Brill depicts "the Unborn growing, pushing into form and shape, and the Old melting reluctantly and with sadness into the ultimate resolution." Brill is represented by the Julia Dohan Gallery in Los Angeles.

ROBERT BRODERSON was born in Connecticut in 1920. His work is found in the collections of the Whitney Museum of American Art, the Wadsworth Atheneum, the Carnegie Institute, and the American Academy of Arts and Letters. "I try to paint people as I see them," he says, "and show the way they feel about life, other people and the world around them." Broderson resides in New York, where his work is represented by the Terry Dintenfass Gallery.

TONY CANGER, who was born in 1940 in Paterson, New Jersey, has completed a mural in Paterson, entitled *Allegory of Good Government.* Canger's canvases, depicting the barren lives of his fellow men, were included in a group exhibition of "new talent" at the Forum Gallery in 1972. He currently teaches at Seton Hall University.

RAFAEL CANOGAR was born in Toledo, Spain in 1934. His work has been exhibited widely throughout Europe, and it is included in the collections of the Carnegie Institute, the Museum of Modern Art, and the Pasadena Art Museum. Canogar intends to present in his canvases "images symbolic of our time as they come to us, adding nothing to them, in favor or against, without critical intention. I try to express the chaos of reality."

SIDNEY CHAFETZ, a printmaker, was born in 1922 in Rhode Island. Chafetz's prints concentrate on politicians, "that group of men upon whose supposed wisdom, good will, and intelligent behavior our very lives depend. It is the subtle relationship between these men and the goals and methods they use in politics that interest me." Chafetz's work is in the collections of the Philadelphia Museum of Art, the Knox Albright Museum, the Butler Institute of American Art, and the Dayton Art Institute. Chafetz presently teaches at Ohio State University in Columbus.

ARTHUR COPPEDGE was born in Brooklyn in 1938. The work of this black artist depicts life on the street and in the home. Coppedge was given his first one-man show at the Acts of Art Gallery, New York, in 1972. His work also appeared in the December, 1971 issue of *Black Enterprise* magazine. Coppedge currently teaches at the Brooklyn Museum Art School.

THOMAS CORNELL was born in Cleveland in 1937. Cornell is Professor of Art at Bowdoin College, where, in 1971, he was given a one-man show of his drawings and prints. Cornell attempts, through the use of evocative subject matter, "not only to admonish people to be more compassionate but to give them something worthy of their compassion." The catalogue of the Bowdoin College exhibition contains many reproductions of Cornell's work.

ELDZIER CORTOR was born in 1916 in Richmond, Virginia. He presently resides in New York. His work has been honored by the Rosenwald Foundation, the Guggenheim Foundation, and the Art Institute of Chicago. Among the books in which Cortor's work is discussed are *American Negro Art,* by Cedric Dover, published by New York Graphic Society, and *17 Black Artists,* by Elton C. Fax, published by Dodd, Mead.

FRANCISCO CORZAS was born in Mexico City in 1936. After finishing his schooling, Corzas traveled throughout Europe and studied for three years in Rome. His sensuous portraits and paintings of street people have been included in several group exhibitions in Mexico, and in many international group shows. Corzas resides in Mexico City.

JACK COUGHLIN was born in Greenwich, Connecticut in 1932. Among the collections in which Coughlin's work can be found are the Metropolitan Museum of Art, the Museum of Modern Art, the

National Collection of Fine Arts in Washington, D.C., and the DeCordova Museum in Massachusetts. In 1970, Aquarius Press published twenty of Coughlin's etchings in a portfolio entitled *Grotesques*. Coughlin is presently Associate Professor of Printmaking and Drawing at the University of Massachusetts.

ROBERT CREMEAN was born in 1932 in Toledo, Ohio. He has had numerous one-man shows. Among the collections in which his work is found are the Detroit Institute of Art, the Los Angeles County Museum of Art, the Santa Barbara Museum of Art, the University of Nebraska in Lincoln, and the University of Miami in Florida.

ROBERT CRUMB, who was born in 1943, discourages biographical information. That's all, folks.

JOSE LUIS CUEVAS was born in 1934 in Triunfo, Mexico. Cuevas's work is found in the collections of the Museum of Modern Art, the Philadelphia Museum of Art, and the Art Institute of Chicago. Among the books Cuevas has illustrated are *Recollections of Childhood,* published by Kanthos Press, Los Angeles, and *Cuevas Por Cuevas,* published by Editorial Era, Mexico, both also written by Cuevas, and *The Worlds of Kafka and Cuevas,* Falcon Press, Philadelphia. Cuevas states that "It is the commonplace world which I have depicted, not in the petty details of daily existence but in its essence." Cuevas lives in Mexico City. His work is represented by the Grace Borgenicht Gallery in New York.

LEONARD CUTROW was born in 1911. He has had several one-man shows, including those at the City of Santa Monica Art Gallery and the Customs House Gallery. In 1967, Cutrow was invited to participate "in United States Navy and Marine Corps activities in South Vietnam in order to paint an art series for the Navy's official art collection." Cutrow's indictments of the brutalities of war are reproduced in *Mankind* magazine, October, 1969. Cutrow lives in Los Angeles.

PETER DEAN, a member of the Rhino Horn group, was born in 1934 in Berlin, and came to the United States four years later. He has exhibited widely, and has been given several one-man shows, most recently at the New Orleans Museum of Art, the Allan Stone Gallery in New York, and the Bienville Gallery in New Orleans. "I am bored with the art-as-decoration scene," states Dean. "I feel that the artist's hand and heart must be exposed in a work of art. I am involved with both the fantasy and reality of my life and times." *Peter Dean: Recent Paintings* was published by the Contemporary Artists Series and the Allan Stone Gallery in 1970.

JOHN DOBBS was born in 1931 in New Jersey. Dobbs, whose work usually concerns itself with political situations, has recently illustrated poems by David Cumberland in a publication entitled *Death and Justice Frescoes*. The April, 1972 issue of *Liberation* magazine also contains reproductions of his work. Dobbs lives in New York, where his work is represented by the A.C.A. Galleries.

DAVID DRIESBACH, a printmaker, was born in 1922 in Wausau, Wisconsin. Among the collections in which his work is found are the Dayton Art Institute, the Columbus Museum, the San Francisco Art Association, the Seattle Art Museum, and the Des Moines Art Center. Driesbach is Associate Professor of Art at Northern Illinois University.

PHILIP EVERGOOD was born in New York in 1901, and was educated in England. He now resides in Bridgewater, Connecticut. In 1960, a retrospective exhibition was held at the Whitney Museum of American Art, and was then circulated to the Walker Art Center, the Wadsworth Atheneum, the Des Moines Art Center, and the San Francisco Museum of Art. Evergood believes that, in time, artists may realize "that a big idea or a poetic idea expressed graphically is nothing to be ashamed of." Evergood's work is represented by the Kennedy Galleries in New York.

OYVIND FAHLSTROM was born in 1928 in São Paulo, Brazil. In 1939, he moved to Sweden, and, in 1961, he came to the United States. He currently lives in New York, and spends some time each year in Sweden. The Sidney Janis Gallery represents his work. Fahlström sees his finished paintings as "somewhere at the point of intersection between paintings, games (of the same type as Monopoly and war games) and puppet shows." A bibliography of Fahlström includes an article written by Torsten Ekbom entitled "Oyvind Fahlström: Models of Shattered Reality," in Art International, Summer, 1966, and the exhibition catalogue of the Fahlström show at the Sidney Janis Gallery, 1971.

MICHAEL FAUERBACH is a native New Yorker, born in 1924. He is a member of the Rhino Horn. "I deal in horror," he has said, "but it is one of recognition, not violence, although sometimes that, too. . . . My people are transition people. They must learn to breathe chemical air and eat processed dinners, and not merely accept them but defend them because it is the price to be paid. What I take perverse pleasure in they must take their only pleasure in."

JOHN FENTON was born in 1912 in Mountaindale, New York. He now resides and works in Woodstock, New York. Among the many one-man shows Fenton has been given was a large exhibition at the Miami Museum in 1971. Fenton expresses his Humanistic orientation as follows: "The whole excruciate effort of the artist is to express in form the content of personal existence." Fenton's metaphysical Humanism is represented by the Babcock Galleries in New York.

ANTONIO FRASCONI, born in Montevideo, Uruguay in 1919, has made the United States his home since 1945. He has received one-man exhibitions at the Terry Dintenfass Gallery in New York, which represents his work, a retrospective exhibition at the Baltimore Museum, and a circulating exhibition organized by the Smithsonian Institution in 1953–54. "The Neighboring Shore," a film featuring over 100 woodcuts by Frasconi, and poems by Walt Whitman, won the Grand Prize at the 1960 Venice Film Festival. Woodcuts by Antonio Frasconi was published in 1958 by E. Weyhe, New York. The exhibition catalogue published by the Baltimore Museum in 1963 is an excellent reference book.

ELIAS FRIEDENSOHN was born in 1924 in New York, where he presently lives. The Roko Gallery in New York, the Feingarten Galleries in Los Angeles, New York, and Chicago, and the Terry Dintenfass Gallery have held one-man shows of Friedensohn's work, and his paintings can be found in the collections of the Whitney Museum of American Art, the Art Institute of Chicago, and the Walker Art Center. Friedensohn's work is currently represented by the Terry Dintenfass Gallery.

REGINALD GAMMON, born in Philadelphia, is Assistant Professor of Art and General Studies at Western Michigan University in Kalamazoo. Gammon's work has been exhibited in group shows at The Studio Museum of Harlem, the Museum of Fine Arts in Boston, the Everson Museum of Art in Syracuse, and the San Francisco Museum of Art. Gammon considers his work "a visual reminder to tell the world of [the black man's] cultural contributions, socially, morally and artistically." The April, 1970 issue of The Art Gallery discusses Gammon's work.

JUAN GENOVES, born in 1930 in Valencia, Spain, now makes Madrid his home. Genoves's work is owned by major museums throughout Europe and the United States, including the Guggenheim Museum and the Museum of Modern Art in New York, the Art Institute of Chicago, the Museum of Modern Art in Rio de Janeiro, the National Gallery in Rome, the Museum of Modern Art in Barcelona, and the Centre National d'Art Contemporain, Paris. His work is represented by the Marlborough Gallery in New York.

PAUL GEORGES was born in Portland, Oregon in 1923. His work is found in the collections of the Museum of Modern Art, the Whitney Museum of American Art, and the New York University and Massachusetts Institute of Technology art collections. Georges values the Humanist intention, but finds that "to say something in art is to risk today." An article by Lawrence Alloway entitled "Paul Georges Paints a Nude" is featured in the February, 1968 issue of *Art News.*

KAHLIL GIBRAN, a sculptor, was born in 1922 in Boston, where he resides. His work has been given one-man shows at the Nordness Galleries in New York, and at the Cambridge Art Association. Gibran describes his subject matter as "man first and foremost, and I am weighted heavily by the sobriety of life as I have seen it." An excellent book in which to view Gibran's sculpture is *Sculpture—Kahlil Gibran,* published in 1970 by The Bartlett Press, Boston.

RUTH GIKOW, born in Russia in 1915, came to the United States at the age of eight. She helped found the American Serigraph Society, and has completed murals in Rockefeller Center and the Bronx State Hospital. Gikow's work primarily deals with people. "Not in the genre sense," she states, "but with my own personal appraisal of the psychic values and encompassing circumstances." Gikow is presently represented by the Forum Gallery in New York. An excellent book in which to see many reproductions of her work is *Ruth Gikow,* published in 1970 by Maecenas Press, Ltd. and Random House, Inc.

GREGORY GILLESPIE was born in 1936 in Roselle Park, New Jersey. He has received several grants, including a Fulbright Fellowship, a National Institute of Arts and Letters grant, and a Tiffany Foundation grant. Gillespie's work is represented by the Forum Gallery in New York, which has recently published a monograph entitled *Gregory Gillespie— Paintings in Italy 1962–70.* Gillespie currently resides in Haydensville, Massachusetts.

LEON GOLUB, Professor of Art at Livingston College, Rutgers University, was born in 1922 in Chicago. He has received many one-man shows in the United States, Europe, and Canada. A retrospective of Golub's work was exhibited at the Tyler School of Art in Philadelphia. Among Golub's writings are "Utopia/anti-Utopia" in *Artforum,* May, 1972, and "The Artist as an Angry Artist," in *Arts,* April, 1967. Insight into the thinking of this often passionate spokesman of Humanist causes can be had in the February, 1970, issue of *Arts* magazine, where Golub is interviewed by Irving Sandler.

LEONEL GONGORA was born in 1932 in Cartago, Colombia. He now lives in New York, and is Professor of Art at Williams College. In 1971, Góngora exhibited, at the Lerner-Heller Gallery, a series of paintings, and an environment, based on the Colombian story of La Maria. The La Maria series was previously exhibited in Colombia, where the government banned its public display. Góngora's intent with this series of works was to create "a trying ground of demystifying a famous romantic work of Colombian literature and of questioning mores, customs, thinking and behavior of Colombian society." Góngora is represented by the Lerner-Heller Gallery in New York.

JAMES GRASHOW was born in 1942 in Brooklyn. Grashow is presently represented by the Allan Stone Gallery in New York, which has given him three one-man shows. Grashow works in woodcuts and graphics, as well as in large papier maché sculptures. Grashow makes his home in New York.

DON GRAY was born in San Francisco in 1935 and currently resides on a farm in Florida, New York. In addition to many one-man shows and group exhibitions around the country, he is art critic for *Applause Magazine.* Of his work he states: "My paintings depict particular individuals with personal characteristics, but they also explore the essence of the human condition, the anger, the despair and perhaps finally, the strength of spirit to continue the eternal struggle to remain human and responsive in the face of societal or cultural forces that would deaden and restrict human development."

BALCOMB GREENE, born in 1904 in Niagara Falls, New York, presently lives and works in New York. His work has been exhibited widely, including one-man shows at the Everhart Museum in Scranton, Pennsylvania, the Phoenix Art Museum, the Santa Barbara Museum of Art, the La Jolla Art Center, and the Adele Bednarz Galleries in Los Angeles. The Whitney Museum of American Art held a retrospective of Greene's work in 1961, which was then circulated throughout the United States by the American Federation of Arts. The catalogue of the retrospective contains many reproductions of his work, and an essay by John I. H. Baur.

RED GROOMS was born in 1937 in Nashville, Tennessee. He presently lives in New York. Grooms's work is represented by the Tibor de Nagy Gallery in New York, where his most recent show was held in 1971. Grooms's work is found in the collections of the Museum of Modern Art, the Art Institute of Chicago, the New School in New York, and the North Carolina Museum of Art in Raleigh.

WILLIAM GROPPER was born in 1897 in New York. His work is represented by the A.C.A. Galleries in New York, where Gropper has had several one-man shows. Among the books reproducing Gropper's work are *Gropper—Collection of Drawings,* published by A.C.A. Galleries, and *The Little Tailor,* published by Dodd, Mead & Co., which Gropper also wrote. In 1968, the A.C.A. Galleries published *William Gropper: Retrospective.* Throughout his career, Gropper has sought to "paint the truth that I feel." Gropper presently lives in Croton-on-Hudson.

CHAIM GROSS was born in 1904 in East Austria. He came to the United States in 1921. He presently resides in New York. Forum Gallery, which represents Gross's work, has given him several one-man shows. Gross was also given a one-man exhibition at the Whitney Museum of American Art, which was circulated throughout the country in 1959. Gross has authored a book entitled *Technique*

of Wood Sculpture, published by Vista House, and a collection of drawings were published under the title *Fantasy Drawings* by Beechhurst Press.

NANCY GROSSMAN states, "Look at those censored faces in the street. You can almost see people saying, 'I'm not going to be caught feeling!'" Grossman was born in 1940 in New York, where she now lives. Her work is represented by Cordier-Ekstrom Gallery in New York, where her last one-woman show was held in 1971.

ROBERT GWATHMEY feels that art "is a desire to find and separate truth from the complex of lies and evasions." The artist believes that pretending "to separate subject matter from artistic intention is to infringe upon the basic structure, to deny its autonomy." Born in 1903 in Richmond, Virginia, Gwathmey now makes his home in Amagansett, Long Island. His work is represented by the Terry Dintenfass Gallery in New York. In 1969, he received a retrospective exhibition at Boston University.

NATHAN CABOT HALE was born in 1925 in California and currently resides in New York. Hale speaks of his role as an artist as "society's extended eye and soul." In order to maintain this role, Hale feels that the artist "lives on the knife edge of civilization." Hale is the author of *Embrace of Life,* published by Harry N. Abrams, Inc., a comprehensive book on the work of sculptor Gustav Vigeland. He has also published a pamphlet entitled *On the Removal of Fig Leaves.* Hale's lyrical Humanist sculptures can be seen at the Midtown Galleries in New York.

DUANE HANSON was born in 1925 in Alexandria, Minnesota. After several years in Germany, Hanson returned to the United States, where he has had several one-man shows. His work is presently represented by O. K. Harris Works of Art in New York, which has given Hanson one-man shows in 1970 and 1972. Hanson, who has little time for obtuse discussions of form and content, sums up his views as follows: "After one works out the form, the artist must ask, 'What have I done?' Then he creates."

MYRON HEISE was born in Bancroft, Nebraska. In the early 1960's, Heise spent several years in Europe, developing his art. Later, he returned to the United States, and he now lives in New York. Heise recently has been painting the activities of 42d Street habitués. These paintings were shown at the Bowery Gallery in New York in a one-man show of Heise's work in 1972.

JOHN HIRSCH was born in 1910 in Philadelphia. He now resides in New York, where he is represented by the Forum Gallery. His one-man shows include a retrospective exhibition at the Philadelphia Art Alliance in 1970. This tenacious opponent of the "art world" has written in the Forum Gallery catalogue of his 1969 show: "A stranger once asked if I was in the entertainment world. I almost said yes, but I thought of my paintings and said, 'No, I make cudgels.' Such self-righteousness makes me squirm but it is a discomfort I live with. It is not easy to stay out of step."

IPOUSTEGUY, born in 1920 in Dun Sur Meuse, now makes his home in Paris. Ipousteguy's sculptures of men metaphorically and physically trapped in situations have been exhibited throughout Europe. In the United States, the Pierre Matisse Gallery in New York exhibits Ipousteguy's work. His work is represented by the Galerie Claude Bernard in Paris.

LUIS JIMENEZ was born in El Paso, Texas in 1940, and now lives in New York. Jimenez feels that art must relate to people, and that "the most neglected element" in art today "is the human one. Art should in some way make a person more aware . . . reflect what it is like to be living in these times and places." Jimenez has had one-man shows at the Graham Gallery in New York, and now is represented by O. K. Harris Works of Art.

LARRY JOHNSON lives in San Francisco. He was born in Lincoln, Nebraska in 1935. Johnson's images of bound and entrapped men have been exhibited in many shows throughout the United States. The Princeton University Art Museum, the San Francisco Art Institute, the Saint Louis Museum, and the Nelson Gallery—Atkins Museum in Kansas City, Missouri are some of the public collections in which Johnson's works are located.

LESTER JOHNSON was born in 1919 in Minneapolis. Previously known for his abstract works, Johnson "went back to nature" in 1954. Since then, Johnson's work has centered on "man and his role in the universe." Johnson makes his figures "complex and not one dimensional." He wants "the men to be part and result of our contemporary world." Johnson's work is represented by the Martha Jackson Gallery in New York. Johnson is the Director of Studies, Graduate Painting, at Yale University, and resides in Milford, Connecticut.

CLIFF JOSEPH, born in Panama in 1922, has lived and worked in New York most of his life. He is a cochairman of the Black Emergency Cultural Coalition. He also works as an art therapist at Lincoln Hospital in the Bronx. His work has been exhibited most recently at a show in the Westbeth Galleries in New York. Joseph works toward creating "a social art, based on my gut perception of our worldy condition." His art "draws upon each viewer to confront himself in consideration of his role in affecting these conditions."

RICHARD KARWOSKI was born in Brooklyn in 1938. Karwoski's work "describes alienation, fear, isolation, self-restrictedness [and] suggests how the city reinforces these self-imposed behavioral patterns." Karwoski presently lives in New York, where he is a member of the Art Department of New York City Community College.

JAMES KEARNS was born in 1924 in Scranton, Pennsylvania. His work has been exhibited widely. Among the books Kearns has illustrated are *Can These Bones Live,* by Edward Dahlberg, published by New Directions, and *The Heart of Beethoven,* by Seldon Rodman, published by Shorewood Press. Kearns perceives the artist "as a human being with a particular talent for revealing himself." Kearns's work is represented by the Sculpture House in New York.

EDWARD KIENHOLZ was born in 1927 in Fairfield, Washington. He now lives outside of Los Angeles. Kienholz has been given one-man exhibitions throughout the United States, including those at the Los Angeles County Museum, the Institute of Contemporary Art in Boston, and the Boise Art Museum. In 1970, a circulating exhibition of his sculptures was sent to major museums in Europe. The catalogue from this exhibition, entitled *Kienholz: Ten Tableaux,* reproduces many of his works, and has an excellent chronology.

WILLIAM KING was born in Jacksonville, Florida in 1925. King's Humanistic sculptures are to be found among several important collections, including the Nelson Rockefeller Collection, the Joseph H. Hirshhorn Collection, and those of New York University, the University of California at Berkeley, and Dartmouth College. King's work is represented by the Terry Dintenfass Gallery in New York.

JOSEPH KINIGSTEIN, a native New Yorker, was born in 1923. He has had several one-man shows at the Nordness Galleries, the Grippi Gallery, and the A.C.A. Galleries, and others. Among the collections in which Kinigstein's work is found are the Museum of Modern Art, the Whitney Museum of American Art, the Butler Art Institute, and the Albright Art Gallery.

CHAIM KOPPELMAN, born in Brooklyn in 1920, is presently Chairman of the Department of Printmaking at the School of Visual Arts in New York. Koppelman feels that his study of Aesthetic Realism with the poet Eli Siegel has been fundamental to his growth as a painter. Using the basic philosophic tenet of Aesthetic Realism, Koppelman's paintings deal with people "as a drama in opposites, among them hiding and showing, cheapness and grandeur, meanness and compassion." The Terrain Gallery in New York, an Aesthetic Realism meeting place, sponsors his work.

JACOB LANDAU was born in 1917 in Philadelphia. He resides in Roosevelt, New Jersey. Landau has been given extensive one-man shows throughout the United States. Among the collections in which Landau's work can be found are the Metropolitan Museum of Art, the Whitney Museum of American Art, the Museum of Modern Art, the National Collection in Washington, D.C., the Los Angeles County Museum, and the Bibliotheque Nationale of Paris. Landau's prints are represented by the Associated American Artists Gallery and his paintings by the Lerner-Heller, both in New York. Landau is one of the most articulate spokesmen for the Humanist intention. His art is based on his contention that, "The art of confrontation with the real, the art of tragic love, of passionate outrage, is both possible and necessary . . . expressing hope and love in the face of terror." The author has published "Tiger of Wrath— Jacob Landau" in *Arts in Society,* Summer, 1971.

MAURICIO LASANSKY was born in Buenos Aires in 1914. In 1943, he received a Guggenheim Fellowship to study in the United States. He has since made his home in Iowa City, Iowa, where he is Professor of Art at the State University of Iowa. In 1960, a retrospective exhibition was organized by the Ford Foundation and circulated throughout the United States. The "Nazi Drawings" have been exhibited at the Philadelphia Museum of Art, the Whitney Museum of American Art, the Des Moines Art Center, and the Palace of Fine Arts in Mexico City. Excellent catalogues of Lasansky's work are *Mauricio Lasansky,* published by the American Federation of Arts, 1960, and *The Nazi Drawings,* published by the Philadelphia Museum of Art in 1966.

JACOB LAWRENCE, a black artist currently residing in New York, was born in New Jersey in 1917. Among his many one-man shows were those at The Studio Museum of Harlem in 1969, the Alan Gallery in 1957 (a retrospective show), and the Terry Dintenfass Gallery, which represents his work. Lawrence has illustrated several books, one of which is *One-Way Ticket,* a book of poetry by Langston Hughes, published by Knopf. Lawrence expresses his Humanist intention this way: "A great purpose of art is to communicate ideas. Color and design are only means to this end."

JUNE LEAF, an artist, was born in 1929 in Chicago. Most recently, Leaf's work has been exhibited at the Museum of Contemporary Art in Chicago in the "Chicago Imagist Art" show. Leaf's work is included in the collections of the Art Institute of Chicago and the Museum of Modern Art, and in the private collection of Herbert Lust of Chicago. Leaf's work is discussed in the June 12, 1972 issue of *Time,* in the review of the "Chicago Imagist Art" show, although her discoveries, and their influence on other artists have yet to be fully recognized. Leaf currently resides in Nova Scotia.

RICO LEBRUN was born in 1900 in Naples, and died in the United States in 1964. His art was shown throughout the United States in one-man shows at major museums and galleries. Throughout his career, he argued against the reluctance of contemporary artists "to look things in the face." The historical importance of this outstanding artist has yet to be fully recognized. One attempt is *Rico Lebrun (1900–1964),* published by the Los Angeles County Museum in 1967, in conjunction with an exhibition of his work. It has a complete biographical chronology of Lebrun's art.

SEYMOUR LEICHMAN was born in 1933 in New York, where he now resides. Most recently, Leichman was given a one-man show at the Kennedy Galleries in New York, which represents his work. Leichman was also honored by a commission from the Government of Jamaica

to create a mural for the city of Kingston. The exhibition catalogue published by the Kennedy Galleries contains excellent reference materials on this artist.

BARBARA LEKBERG was born in 1925 in Portland, Oregon. Among the several one-woman shows she has had are those held at Fairfield University in Connecticut, and the Museums of Fine Arts in Birmingham, Alabama and Columbia, South Carolina. Lekberg's concern in her work is to show "within discord, a structure which has order, a shape which is moving and serene at once."

BIRNEY LETTICK was born in 1919 in New Haven, Connecticut. Lettick's work is represented by Graham Gallery in New York, where he received a one-man show in 1970. His work can be found in the collections of Yale University, Time, Inc., and the National Geographic Society. Several of Lettick's works are reproduced in the catalogue of his show at the Graham Gallery. Lettick is the founder of the New Haven Workshop, and is presently acting as its Director.

DAVID LEVINE states, "I am the present," who perceives himself as "a sensitized creature viewing the world, and [my art] is my statement to it." Levine's vivid caricatures can be found in the *New York Review of Books.* In 1971, Levine took part in a two-man exhibition at the Brooklyn Museum, where he exhibited many of his paintings. A catalogue published by the Museum reproduced several of these works, and a collection of Levine's drawings were published in *A Summer Sketchbook,* by Mitchell Press. Levine, who presently lives in Brooklyn, was born in 1926. The Forum Gallery in New York represents Levine's work.

JACK LEVINE, born in 1915 in Boston, resides in New York. Levine's work has been exhibited in one-man shows throughout the United States and Europe. Included in this long list are retrospective exhibitions at the Institute of Contemporary Art in Boston, the DeCordova Museum, and the Whitney Museum of American Art, and other one-man shows in

Puerto Rico, Rome, and Mexico City. Levine's work, which can be found in the collections of the major museums in the United States, is presently represented by the Kennedy Galleries in New York. Levine sees his concern with painting people in their situations as "the most taxing problem an artist can set himself to do."

MENAHEM LEWIN was born in Palestine in 1918, and grew up in Brooklyn, where he now lives. Lewin perceives the role of the contemporary artist as the vehicle for expressing the conscience of man. Lewin has found, however, "that this is not a pleasant image to hang on the wall. Man does not ordinarily want to confront his innermost self." Lewin is Associate Professor of Art at New York City Community College.

RICHARD LINDNER was born in Hamburg, Germany, in 1901. He moved to France in 1933, and then, when war broke out, came to the United States in 1941. He currently lives in New York. His many one-man shows include several at the University Art Gallery in Berkeley, and several more at the Cordier-Ekstrom Gallery in New York, which represents his work. His work is owned by the Whitney Museum of American Art, the Museum of Modern Art, the Cleveland Museum of Art, and the Tate Gallery in London.

ANTONIO LOPEZ-GARCIA was born in Tomelloso, Spain in 1936, and now lives in Madrid. He has had one-man shows throughout Spain, and several in the United States, including one at the Staempfli Gallery in New York. John Canaday discussed Lopez-Garcia's work in an article entitled "Throw Away that Incubator" in the *New York Times,* November 16, 1968. Lopez-Garcia's work is presently represented by the Marlborough Gallery in New York.

BORIS LURIE was born in 1924 in Leningrad. Lurie was involved in the cooperative gallery movement in the early 1960's, and had several shows at the 10th Street Gallery during that time. "No is an In-volvement" by Michelle Stuart appeared in the September, 1963 issue of *Artforum.* Lurie resides in New York.

GIACOMO MANZU was born in Bergamo, Italy in 1908. Manzu's lyrical Humanism can be found in the collections of the National Gallery of Art in Rome, the Museum of Modern Art, and the Tate Gallery. *Manzu,* by John Rewald and published by New York Graphic Society, contains excellent material on his work. Manzu resides outside of Rome, Italy.

MARISOL was born in Paris in 1930. Her work is found in the collections of the Whitney Museum of American Art, the Albright Art Gallery, the Arts Club of Chicago, and the Museum of Modern Art. Marisol presently resides in New York, where her work is represented by the Sidney Janis Gallery.

TONY MARTIN was born in 1937 in Knoxville, Tennessee. Martin says he paints places where "characteristics of our condition can collect. Enigma and predicament as they reside in an element or in a space. . . . Amalgam being, man summing himself in one or another figuration, faced with his own habits." Martin also composes various intermedia programs. This aspect of his work combines light, sound, movement, and works in a unique involvement of technology and Humanist intention. Martin currently resides in New York.

ROBERT MARX, born in Nordheim, Germany in 1925, came to the United States in 1927. He is Professor of Art at the State University College at Brockport, New York. Marx's prints are represented by Associated American Artists Gallery in New York, and by the Schuman Gallery in Rochester. Among the collections in which Marx's work is found are the Museum of Modern Art, the Philadelphia Museum of Art, the Whitney Museum of American Art, and the Los Angeles County Museum of Art.

MARYAN S. MARYAN was born in Poland in 1927. Between 1939 and 1945, Maryan was held in Nazi concentration camps in Poland. He later lived in Israel and in Paris. In 1962, Maryan came to the United States, and made New York his home. Among the many publications of his work include illustrations for *The Trial,* by Franz Kafka; *La Managerie Humaine,* a collection of 40 drawings published by the Editions Tisné in Paris; and linoleum cuts and lithographs, both published by the Allan Frumkin Gallery in New York.

RALPH MASSEY says, "If I were asked to characterize the entire history of mankind in a word, I would have to call it grotesque." Born in Detroit in 1938, and now living in Los Angeles, Massey has been creating a commentary of contemporary man through his sculptures. They have been exhibited in one-man shows at the Downey Museum of Art, the Sawyer Gallery in San Francisco, the Feingarten Gallery in Los Angeles, and at the Gallery Del Sol in Santa Barbara.

JAY MILDER was born in 1934 in Omaha, Nebraska. He now resides in New York. Milder has exhibited in group shows with the Rhino Horn, and has had several one-man shows. He has written that his method in both his painting and sculpture is Cabalistic in that "I work in a state of non-thinking in revelation doing away with my intellect." The exhibition catalogue published by the Museum of Norfolk in 1972 is an excellent reference to Milder's work.

PETER MILTON, born in Lower Merion, Pennsylvania in 1930, now resides and works in Francestown, New Hampshire. His prints have been exhibited widely. Recently, Aquarius Press published a series of prints illustrating William James's *The Jolly Corner. Etchings by Peter Milton,* published by the DeCordova Museum, is an excellent catalogue for further reference.

ALICE NEEL, who was recently awarded an honorary Doctor of Fine Arts degree from Moore College of Art, and was given a retrospective there the same year, was born in Merion Square, Pennsylvania in 1908. Presently represented by Graham Gallery in New York, Neel's work is found in the collections of the Museum of Modern Art, the American Museum in Moscow, and the Dillard Institute in New Orleans. Neel feels that her world "has been swept away. And yet I can't think that the human creature will be forever *verboten.*" A feature article about Neel's work was written by Jack Kroll, and appeared in *Newsweek* on January 31, 1966.

GLADYS NILSSON was born in Chicago in 1940. Nilsson was a member of the Hairy Who. Among the collections in which her art is found are the Museum of Modern Art, the Whitney Museum of American Art, the Art Institute of Chicago, Illinois State University, and Southern Illinois University. Nilsson's work is discussed and reproduced in the June 12, 1972 issue of *Newsweek,* in a review of the exhibition entitled "Chicago Imagist Art." Nilsson presently resides in Sacramento, California. Her work is represented by the Phyllis Kind Gallery in Chicago.

BRIAN NISSEN, born in England in 1939, has made his home in Mexico City since 1963. His work has been shown in Puerto Rico, and in several exhibitions in Mexico City. Nissen believes art is not "something to beautify or decorate . . . or to amuse or entertain us." Nissen feels that art must become an activity in which each person, to his own degree, "can fulfill and direct his life," while accepting that "there might not be any special meaning or grand design in it."

JIM NUTT was born in 1938 in Pittsfield, Massachusetts. Nutt was a member of the Hairy Who. Nutt's work is represented by the Phyllis Kind Gallery in Chicago, where he has been given two one-man shows. Nutt's work is found in the collections of the Metropolitan Museum of Art, the Whitney Museum of American Art, and the Art Institute of Chicago. The catalogue of the "Chicago Imagist Art" show of 1972 is a good reference for more information on Nutt's work. Nutt presently lives in Sacramento, California.

ELLIOT OFFNER was born in Brooklyn in 1931. His work is represented by the Forum Gallery, where he has had several one-man shows. Offner's work can be found in the collections of the Brooklyn Museum, the Metropolitan Museum of Art, the Victoria and Albert Museum in England, and the Slater Museum. Offner is Professor of Art at Smith College, and Director of the Rosemary Press.

BERNARD OLSHAN, who was born in New York in 1921, is presently Director of the Art Department at the Mosholu-Montefiore Community Center in the Bronx. Olshan's metaphysical Humanism has been exhibited at Syracuse University, the University of Miami, Hofstra University, the Roko Gallery, and the A.C.A. Galleries.

GASTON ORELLANA was born in 1933 in Valparaiso, Chile. He became a Spanish citizen in 1951, and he currently lives in Madrid and in Milan. Orellana has received an invitation to participate in an exhibition of Spanish painters, organized in honor of Picasso, entitled "La Paloma," which will be shown at the Vandres Gallery in Madrid in 1973. Among the collections where Orellana's work can be found are the Metropolitan Museum of Art, the Delgado Museum, the Museum of Fine Arts in Phoenix, the Museum of Modern Art of São Paolo, Brazil, the National Museum of Fine Arts, Santiago, and the Museum of Contemporary Arts in Barcelona. Orellana wants "the stigma of war and its goals . . . the horrible presence of aggressive armament . . . and the great multitudes that run on the streets . . . to live on the white canvas of each work."

ED PASCHKE was born in 1937 in Chicago, where he presently resides. Paschke's one-man shows include those at the Deson-Zaks Gallery in Chicago, and at the Hundred Acres Gallery in New York. Both galleries represent his work. In 1973, Paschke will be given circulating exhibitions in Canada and England. A discussion of Paschke's work can be found in the April/May issue of *Chicago* magazine, and in the June 12, 1972 issue of *Newsweek* magazine.

PETER PASSUNTINO, a member of the Rhino Horn group, was born in 1936 in Chicago. Passuntino has said that it makes little difference to him if he "underlines struggle or parenthesizes happiness. I cannot capsulize my painting to fit the mood of an art-minded audience. I am more interested in discovering the underlying root of the things in my world and transferring them into a painting language." Passuntino presently resides in New York.

PHILIP PEARLSTEIN was born in 1924 in Pittsburgh. He has received many one-man exhibitions throughout the United States. In 1970, he received a retrospective exhibition at Vassar College in Poughkeepsie, New York. In an article entitled "Why I Paint the Way I Do," for the *New York Times,* August 22, 1971, Pearlstein described his particular kind of realism: "As a rose is a rose, so my paintings of models are paintings of models. . . . I can only hope to project my respect for their persons by depicting them as accurately as possible. That involves seeing every part of their body." Pearlstein is presently represented by the Allan Frumkin Gallery in New York.

MICHAEL PETERS, born in 1943 in Brooklyn, now works and lives in San Francisco. He has participated in several group shows throughout the country. His work is represented in the collections of critic Henry Seldis, Molly Barnes, and the San Francisco Museum of Art. Peters's paintings capture the moment when "we stand balanced between our 'internal' (what we believe to be true) and 'external' (what is real) realities."

JOSEPH RAFFAEL, born in 1933 in Brooklyn, now makes his home in San Geronimo, California. "I do feel," Raffael wrote in a letter to the author, "that the art thing is essential to my nature and my being, but that the life is far greater than the art." Raffael teaches at Sacramento State College. An excellent source for viewing of Raffael's work is the catalogue published in 1970 by the Reese Palley Gallery entitled *Joseph Raffael.*

ANTON REFREGIER, born in Russia in 1905, went to live in Paris in 1920, and subsequently moved to the United States, where he now makes his home. He is consultant on the mural programs for the governments of Guatemala and Puerto Rico. In 1972, he received a retrospective exhibition at the 1199 Gallery in New York. His other one-man exhibitions include retrospective shows in Russia—at the Museum of Fine Arts, Moscow, and the Hermitage. Refregier has authored many books, including *Natural Figure Drawing,* published by Tudor Press, and *An Artist's Journey,* published by International Publishers.

JOYCE REOPEL was born in Worcester, Massachusetts in 1933. She has had one-woman shows in Boston at the Boris Mirski Gallery and the Tragos Gallery. Reopel's work is included in the collections of the Fogg Art Museum, the Pennsylvania Academy of Fine Arts, and Ohio State University. Reopel currently teaches at Wheaton College.

FAITH RINGGOLD, who has been involved in numerous cultural and political activities, was born in 1934 in New York. Ringgold sees artists "as the only element within society which can actually afford to tell the truth." Black artists, she feels, "must refer to the black experience . . . if they are to tell the truths as blacks." Ringgold has had several one-woman shows in New York, and has recently completed a mural at the Women's House of Detention in New York. She presently teaches at both Wagner College and the Bank Street College. An article on Ringgold's work appeared in the April, 1970 issue of *Art in America* magazine.

MANUEL 'SPAIN' RODRIGUEZ, who was born in 1940, presently resides in San Francisco. In a letter to the author, this artist has written: "Art is essentially the communication of feeling or idea from one person to others via some media. Even with its limited facilities the underground comic industry produced a minimum of 10,000 copies per issue. What art gallery can reach that many people? Against this fact the only arguments they can muster are essentially snobbishly arrogant and elitist. I feel the time is at hand when comic art will be given the critical appreciation it deserves and I am happy to aid any effort to bring this about."

MARK ROGOVIN was born in Buffalo, New York in 1946. Currently living in Chicago, Rogovin has been instrumental in creating several mural projects throughout the city. Rogovin recently opened the Public Art Workshop for students of Columbia College, Chicago. Rogovin has studied muralism with Siqueiros in Mexico, and has made murals his primary artistic concern. He often expresses his wish that those in all other cultural fields "look at their own work and question how they can become a meaningful vehicle for reaching others."

SEYMOUR ROSOFSKY was born in Chicago in 1924. He is Acting Chairman of the Art Department of the City College of Chicago. He has had numerous one-man shows, including those at the Feigen Gallery, Chicago, and the Galerie du Dragon, Paris. Both these galleries represent Rosofsky's work, as well as the Graphics Gallery in San Francisco and the Phyllis Kind Gallery in Chicago.

MAHLER RYDER, born in Columbus, Ohio, in 1937, resides in Providence, Rhode Island, where he teaches at the Rhode Island School of Design. For several years, Ryder lived in Germany, where he had three one-man shows. Ryder's series of works based on New York subway riders responds to his perceptions that, "It is in the subways that the majority of New Yorkers get together." For further reading on Ryder's work, refer to articles in the May, 1971 issue of *Print* magazine, and a review in the *New York Times,* February 1, 1969.

PETER SAUL states, "I will show people that what they want to look at is not the kind of thing they will enjoy seeing." Born in 1934 in San Francisco, Saul presently lives in Mill Valley, California. Saul's work is represented by the Allan Frumkin Gallery, which has given him several one-man shows. He has received exhibitions in Paris, Rome, and Turin, and is in the collections of Oberlin College, the Museum of Modern Art, and the Art Institute of Chicago.

ALFONSE SCHILLING resides in New York. He works primarily in a photographic medium, usually kinetic, and his work does not easily lend itself to reproduction. In his piece on the Chicago convention, and in his many works of Humanistic portraiture and reportage, Schilling demonstrates a unique approach to the realization of the Humanist intention.

ED SCHLINSKI was born in Boston in 1920. Currently working and living in Roosevelt, New Jersey, Schlinski's sculptures of the absurd reflect his own view of life, from which, he states, "among other things, you could damn near die laughing." Schlinski is a self-taught artist, whose work is represented by the Lerner-Heller Gallery, which gave him his first one-man show in 1972.

AUBREY SCHWARTZ was born in 1928. He currently resides in Friendsville, Pennsylvania. The Kanthos Press published a series of lithographs entitled *A Bestiary,* and the Gehenna Press published *Predatory Birds,* another series of lithographs, in 1958. Schwartz's work is included in the collections of the Brooklyn Museum, the Metropolitan Museum of Art, the Philadelphia Museum of Art, the Art Institute of Chicago, and the Minneapolis Institute of Arts. Schwartz is interested in his subjects as "human beings—who they are and why; where they are going; their relationship to society and to man."

REINER SCHWARZ, born in Hirshberg, Germany in 1940, now lives in Berlin. His prints have been exhibited throughout Germany. In the United States, Schwarz's prints are represented by the Associated American Artists Gallery in New York.

ARTHUR SECUNDA, presently represented by the Associated American Artists Gallery, was born in 1927 in New

Jersey. Secunda has also worked as a writer and critic for *Arts* magazine. Secunda's work is included in the collections of the Museum of Modern Art, the Smithsonian Institution, the National Collection of Fine Arts in Washington, D.C., the Brooklyn Museum, as well as many museums in Europe.

GEORGE SEGAL was born in 1924 in New York. Segal's sculptures can be found in the permanent collections of the Museum of Modern Art, the Whitney Museum of American Art, the Walker Art Museum, the Stedejilk Museum, the Art Institute of Chicago, and the Art Gallery of Toronto. The artist states his interest is in the "series of shocks and encounters that a person can have moving through space and around several objects placed in careful relationships." The catalogue of Segal's show at the Sidney Janis Gallery in 1971 reproduces many of Segal's sculptures.

ANTONIO SEGUI was born in Cordoba, Argentina in 1934. He now makes his home in Paris, where his work is represented by the Galerie Claude Bernard. His art has been exhibited throughout Europe and South America. In the United States, his work is represented by the Lefebre Gallery in New York, which gave him a one-man show in 1972.

BEN SHAHN was born in Lithuania in 1898 and came to the United States in 1906. At the time of his death in 1969, Shahn's work was exhibited widely throughout the world. Throughout his career, Shahn attempted to clarify and elaborate his Humanist intention. His book, *The Shape of Content,* is his best known statement. Of the importance of intention itself towards an appreciation of art, Shahn has written: "The very act of making a painting is an intending one . . . the value of man, if he has any at all, resides in his intention, in the degree to which he has moved away from the brute, in his intellect at its peak and in his humanism at its peak."

PHILIP SHERROD, born in 1935 in Pauls Valley, Oklahoma, now resides in New

York. He has had a one-man show at the Sonraed Gallery, and his work is represented in the collections of the Tulane University Museum and the Everhart Museum. Sherrod's view, expressed to the author, is that "there is a profound lack of personal investigation in art today." Reproductions of Sherrod's work can be found in *Sherrod,* the catalogue of his exhibition at the Sonraed Gallery, 1971.

SIDNEY SIMON was born in 1917 in Pittsburgh. He lives in New York, where his work is represented by the Graham Gallery. Simon's art has always centered around "man and his mores, syndromes, psychology and more so, story-telling." Simon has found the repercussions of this orientation, however, to be "very risky business as far as art is concerned."

SYLVIA SLEIGH was born in England, and came to the United States in 1961. In 1962, she settled in New York, where she currently resides. Sleigh has had several one-woman shows, including a 1972 show at the Lerner-Heller Gallery, which represents her work. The exhibition catalogue contains an essay by John Russell.

MOSES SOYER was born in 1899 in southern Russia, and came to the United States in 1913. Presently living in New York, he has had many one-man shows. Soyer has authored *Painting the Human Figure,* published in 1969 by Watson Guptill, and has illustrated *First Book of Ballet* by Noel Streitfield, published by Franklyn Watts Publishing Company. Among the many volumes reproducing his work is *Moses Soyer,* published by World Publishing Co., which contains essays by Philip Evergood and Charlotte Willard. Soyer's work is represented by A.C.A. Galleries.

RAPHAEL SOYER, born in 1899, is committed to the view that "if art is to survive, it must describe and express people, their lives and times. It must communicate." Among his many one-man shows is a retrospective exhibition, held at the Whitney Museum of Art in 1967, which traveled to art centers in the major cities

of the United States. Among the books Soyer has written are *A Painter's Pilgrimage: An Account of a Journey,* published by Crown Press, with drawings by the author, and *Homage to Thomas Eakins, Etc.,* published by Thomas Yoseloff. An excellent reference to Soyer's work is the catalogue from the Whitney exhibition. *Raphael Soyer,* written by Lloyd Goodrich, published by Abrams in 1973. Soyer's work is represented by the Forum Gallery.

NICHOLAS SPERAKIS was born in 1943 in New York, where he currently resides. He has received honors for both his paintings and his graphic work. A member of the Rhino Horn, his work is found in the collections of the Brooklyn Museum, the Philadelphia Museum of Art, and the Museum of Arts and Sciences in Norfolk, Virginia. Sperakis employs his experiences of New York to create on canvas his vision of contemporary life as "an insane episode from a Marx Brothers' comedy staged by the Marquis de Sade."

NANCY SPERO was born in Cleveland, and presently lives in New York. She has received one-woman shows at the University of California at San Diego, and at the Galerie Breteau in Paris. Spero has written several articles, among them, "Women's Speak-out," in the *New York Element,* February–March, 1972, and "The Whitney Museum and Women," *Art Gallery Magazine,* January, 1971. Spero expresses her commitment to the Humanist intention in this way: "I intend an art of near insane ferocity. The forms are fractured, spontaneous, existential."

J. L. STEG, Professor of Art at Tulane University, was born in 1922 in Virginia. Steg's prints have been purchased by the Brooklyn Museum, the Dallas Museum, and The Print Club of Philadelphia. Steg sees the handmade, hand-pulled print "as a defiance of the machine—an anachronism with the aura of intimacy." Steg's prints are represented by the Associated American Artists Gallery in New York, the Franz Bader Gallery in Washington, D.C., and the Glade Gallery in New Orleans.

SAUL STEINBERG was born in 1914 in Rumania. He came to the United States in 1942, and presently lives in New York. Among the many collections where Steinberg's works can be found are the Albright Museum, the Institute of Art in Detroit, the Metropolitan Museum of Art, the Museum of Modern Art, the Victoria and Albert Museum, and Harvard University. Steinberg's cartoons have been published in *The Art of Living* by Harper and Brothers. His cartoons are most known through their appearance in the *New Yorker* magazine. Steinberg feels that, "Everything has a message, even the smell of museums. In Europe, museums smell of town halls and grade schools; in America, they smell like banks." The Sidney Janis Gallery in New York represents Steinberg's work.

MAY STEVENS, born in Boston in 1924, now works and lives in New York. She has received ten one-woman shows in New York, Paris, and Washington, D.C. Among the collections in which her work is included are the Whitney Museum of American Art, Washington University in St. Louis, the Jacksonville Museum in Florida, the University of Miami, and the Schenectady Museum. Vitality is one of the things Stevens looks for in art: "Not only a human statement, but the very presence of human striving, thinking, feeling, a paradigm of what it means to live." She feels that "art which is based on formula—marinated—is art's opposite."

JAMES STROMBOTNE, who wants his work to be "as specific as hell, but enigmatic, too," was born in 1934 in Watertown, South Dakota. He has received one-man exhibitions from the San Jose State College, the Bertha Schaefer Gallery in New York, the Capper Gallery in San Francisco, and the Jodi Scully in Los Angeles, where his work is currently represented. In 1961, Phelan and Co. published Strombotne's illustrations of Dostoevsky's *The Brothers Karamazov* in a folio of 500 editions.

MICHELLE STUART was born in Los Angeles, and now resides in New York.

Stuart's sculpted portraits have been exhibited widely in Paris and in Mexico City. In 1968, several of Stuart's drawings were published by the Cape Goliard Press in London, with poems by Paul Blackburn. In 1963, Stuart published an article entitled "No Is an Involvement" in *Artforum* magazine.

PAUL THEK was born in 1933 in Brooklyn. He has received one-man shows at the Pace Gallery in New York, the Stedejilk Museum in Amsterdam, the National Museum in Stockholm, and the Galleria 88 in Rome. Thek's work is represented by the Thelen Gallery in Cologne. He currently resides in Amsterdam, where he creates his environmental sculpture.

RUSS THOMPSON was born in Jamaica, West Indies. He now resides in New York. His first one-man exhibition was held in 1972, at the Crane-Korchin Gallery in New York. Thompson's work has been shown in group exhibitions at the Museum of Modern Art, the Smithsonian Institution, the Boston Museum of Fine Arts, and the New Jersey State Museum. His work is in the collections of artist Benny Andrews, Curator Carroll Greene, the Frederick Douglas Institute in Washington, D.C., and the City of Atlantic City, New Jersey.

GEORGE TOOKER, who presently makes his home in Hartland, Vermont, was born in 1920 in Brooklyn. His work can be found in the permanent collections of the Museum of Modern Art, the Whitney Museum of American Art, and the Metropolitan Museum of Art. Tooker would like "to express man's relation to the world and to himself—and to some spiritual force outside himself." Tooker's work is represented by the Frank Rehn Galleries in New York.

JOYCE TREIMAN, born in Evanston, Illinois in 1922, now lives in Pacific Palisades, California. Presently represented by the Forum Gallery, Treiman has received several one-woman shows. People have always been the major subject matter of Treiman's work, in contrast to what she sees as the major tendency in art today: "To pluck one thing out of a painting and blow it up to the proportions of a major conceptual idea." Treiman calls this "left-nostril painting."

ERNEST TROVA, a self-taught artist, was born in 1927 in St. Louis, where he currently resides. His sculptures and prints of mechanical man have been exhibited throughout the United States and in Europe, and are represented by the Pace Gallery, New York. "I value detachment," Trova once stated. He manifests this detachment in the cold and alienated men he creates. *Trova: Selected Works 1953–66,* published by the Pace Gallery, is an excellent source for further viewing of Trova's works.

RENZO VESPIGNANI was born in 1924. He presently lives in Rome. Among the many one-man shows Vespignani has received are those held at the Galleria Forni in Bologna, the Galleria dei Lanza in Milan, the Landau Gallery in Los Angeles, and the Galleria Il Fante di Spade in Rome, where his work is represented. Many excellent reproductions of Vespignani's work can be seen in the catalogue published by the Galleria Il Fante di Spade.

PETER WALKER was born in 1946 in New York, where he currently resides. Walker has had one-man shows at the Terry Dintenfass Gallery, which represents his work, and at the Gallery Quadrante. Walker says he tries to paint the pictures he wants to see: "I'd like," he has written, "to see rooms full of paintings (not hygienic temples) that jumped with reflections, references, and illusions." He thinks a good painter "still can look at an object, a place or a person and discover things. I'd like to be a magician."

WILLIAM WEEGE, born in 1935 in Milwaukee, resides in Chicago. Weege's prints, many of them farcical depictions of the myths of political life, have been exhibited throughout the country. Weege's work is represented at the Associated American Artists Gallery and the Blue Parrot Gallery, both in New York. Among the collections in which Weege's work is found are the Akron Art Institute, the Art Institute of Chicago, the Museum of Mod-

ern Art, the Philadelphia Museum of Art, the San Francisco Museum of Art, and the Brooklyn Museum.

ELBERT WEINBERG was born in 1928 in Hartford, Connecticut. Weinberg feels that his work attempts "to find forceful images, freshly seen, that will reach out and touch another sensibility." Weinberg currently lives in Boston, and is represented by the Grace Borgenicht Gallery in New York.

CHARLES WELLS was born in New York in 1935. He now lives in Vermont. Wells's work has been exhibited in one-man shows at the Hinckley-Brohel Galleries in New York and Washington, D.C., and at the FAR Gallery, where his work is represented. The Summer, 1964 issue of the *Massachusetts Review* contains an article on the sculpture of this metaphysical Humanist.

CHARLES WHITE was born in 1918 in Chicago. White's one-man shows include those at the Forum Gallery, and at the Heritage Gallery in Los Angeles, which represents his work. White's work takes shape "within the vortex of a black experience," and demonstrates his belief that "the people of this land cannot always be insensible to the dictates of justice or deaf to the voice of humanism." An excellent book for reference is *Images of Dignity—The Drawings of Charles White,* published by the Heritage Press, 1967. White presently resides in California.

HIRAM WILLIAMS, born in 1917 in Indianapolis, Indiana, lives in Gainsville, Florida, where he is Professor of Art at the University of Florida. Author of *Notes for a Young Painter,* published in 1963 by Prentice-Hall, Williams has written that "the painter is always about one thing: he is busy creating a world which, while acting as a mirror to man's experience in the real world, also behaves as an autonomous world of form." Williams's work is represented by the Nordness Galleries in New York, where he has been given several one-man shows.

S. CLAY WILSON was born in San Francisco in 1941. Like other cartoonists, he shies away from the biographical. He was instrumental in the comic book movement, and in alerting the author to quite a few very talented artists. He resides in San Francisco.

JAN WITTENBER currently resides in Chicago, where he is a staff member of the DuStable Museum of African American History. The only white staff member of the museum, Wittenber has been recognized for his contribution to the continuing dissemination of African American History. At the Dixon State School for mentally retarded children, he organized "Drawings for Dixon," by obtaining art works from artists throughout Illinois for the school's interior walls. Wittenber expresses the Humanistic potential of art as follows: "Novelty is a substitute for art or truth. Artists should not be ashamed to be human. Art should be integrated with life."

MELVIN ZABARSKY, Professor of Art at the University of New Hampshire, was born in Worcester, Massachusetts in 1932. He describes the narrative approach of his unusual portraiture as the result "of the actual physical interaction of image and form. The content of the narrative is 20th century history." The catalogue of Zabarsky's exhibition at the DeCordova Museum is a good reference for further information on this artist. His work can be found in the collections of the Museum of Modern Art, the DeCordova Museum, the Addison Gallery of American Art, and the Currier Gallery of Art in Manchester, Massachusetts.

NOTES

1. R. Buckminster Fuller, *Utopia or Oblivion: The Prospects for Humanity* (New York: Bantam, 1969).
2. Marcel Duchamp, as quoted in Edward Lucie–Smith, *Late Modern: The Visual Arts Since 1945* (New York: Praeger, 1969), p. 11.
3. While there have been many books and articles analyzing the relationship between modernism and modern science, two of the most interesting are *Loss of Self in Modern Literature and Art,* by Wylie Sypher (New York: Random House, 1964), and *Behind Appearance,* by L. H. Waddington (Cambridge: MIT Press, 1969).
4. The modernist exploration of the technological environment, and the Humanist's concern with its impact on human life, are not to be construed as exclusive categories. In fact, the greater body of artists' work reflect both concerns in varying degrees. I have used these classifications as convenient tools for describing artists who clearly emphasize one of the concerns as the central feature of their work. There are, of course, numerous examples of overlap: Humanists who reveal prominent formalistic concerns, and formalists whose art is motivated by Humanist intentions. Space does not permit discussion of the work of Picasso, the Dadaists, and the early Surrealists, who excelled in both formal innovation and major Humanist statements. Yet, these classifications, if understood as generalities, are worthwhile, particularly since World War II, when the separations became very apparent.
5. There could be some objection to my inclusion of Pop Art in this category. In addition to the points I raise on page 49, I would add only that, while much Pop Art did refer to technological development and its impact, Pop Art minimized the importance of the tension that was sometimes its subject matter. But this point can not be said to apply generally to the works of, say, Oldenburg, who might have been included in this book among the absurdists.
6. Ernst Fischer, *The Necessity of Art: A Marxist Approach* (Middlesex: Penguin, 1963), p. 216.
7. Fyodor Dostoevsky, *Notes from Underground and "The Grand Inquisitor"* New York: E. P. Dutton, 1960), p. 128.
8. *Ibid.,* p. 138.
9. The inaccuracies are far too numerous to be given adequate attention here. In fact, the history of Humanism in this century has itself suffered from minimal attention. The historical importance of such diverse artists as Ernst Barlach, Kathe Kollwitz, George Grosz, John Heartfield, Edvard Munch, and Oscar Kokoschka to the Humanist tradition has been overlooked as part of a larger misunderstanding of Expressionism, which is wrongly treated exclusively as a style, rather than as a particular manifestation of Humanist intention. Similarly, the influential works of Max Beckmann, James Ensor, Alberto Giacometti, Georges Rouault, many of the Surrealists, particularly Matta, and all the German Expressionists, have not been seen as part of the Humanist whole. Because the formalists believe that newer movements make older ones obsolete, they have failed to recognize that many 'superceded" forms are still vital, and, when combined with fresh and original content, they make for the creation of excellent works of art.

Even discussions of the work of Picasso generally fail to consider both the large body of his work that attempts to advance form, and seminal works, such as *Guernica, The Charnel House,* and *Massacre in Korea,* which are his finest Humanist statements, utilizing the developments found in earlier work. Such discussions also do little justice to Picasso's earlier Blue and Rose periods.

The Mexican muralists, and particularly Orozco, who is one of the great artists of this century, have also not been seen in the context of the Humanist tradition. Finally, such outstanding artists as Rico Lebrun and Philip Evergood, who both have had wide impact on the development of Humanist art in our time, have not been given the recognition they deserve.

The refusal of formalists to recognize and deal with the Humanist tradition as an ongoing development within art history explains many of the contradictions to be found in their treatment of contemporary artists. Thus, while Richard Lindner, for example, demonstrated a vigorous commitment to the creation of Humanist works for over two decades, it was only when

Pop Art was made into a fashion that his work suddenly became valued by critics and historians, who had previously shown critical indifference to his creations.

10. As I indicated in the Introduction, the works discussed and presented here represent a fraction of the work deserving attention. Further, in my attention to clarify the general misconceptions concerning Humanism, I could not deal with the specific wrongs perpetrated on individual artists. I feel that a very worthwhile book to consult here is *The Indignant Eye,* by Ralph E. Shikes (Beacon, 1969). The book has numerous examples of the work of Humanist printmakers, and a reasonably adequate treatment of a number of historical figures prominent in the development of the Humanist tradition.

11. Irving Sandler, *The Triumph of American Painting: A History of Abstract Expressionism* (New York: Praeger, 1970), p. 1.

12. Harold Rosenberg, *The Anxious Object: Art Today and Its Audience* (New York: Mentor, 1969), p. 46.

13. Sandler, *The Triumph of American Painting,* p. 1.

14. *Ibid.,* p. 31.

15. Herbert Read, *Art and Alienation* (New York: Horizon, 1967), p. 24.

16. George W. Morgan, *The Human Predicament: Dissolution and Wholeness* (New York: Dell, 1970), p. 10.

17. Edgar Wind*, Art and Anarchy* (New York: Vintage, 1969), p. 20.

18. Richard Anuskiewicz, as quoted by Rosenberg, *The Anxious Object,* p. 47.

19. Lucie-Smith, *Late Modern,* p. 273.

20. Kenneth Clark, "The Blot and the Diagram," *Encounter* (January, 1963), p. 32.

21. Clive Bell, *Art* (New York: Capricorn, 1958), p. 160.

22. Read, *Art and Alienation, p.* 8.

23. Rensselaer W. Lee, *Ut Pictura Poesis: The Humanistic Theory of Painting* (New York: W. W. Norton, 1967), p. 9.

24. Etienne Gilson, *Painting and Reality,* The A. W. Mellon Lectures in the Fine Arts (New York: Pantheon Books for the Bollinger Foundation, 1957), p. 243.

25. Herbert Read, *Art Now* (New York: Harcourt, Brace & Company, 1934), pp. 52–53.

26. Bertolt Brecht, as quoted by Herbert Marcuse, *One Dimensional Man* (London: Sphere, 1968), p. 65.

27. Karl Marx, as quoted by Herbert Marcuse, "Art as a Form of Reality," in Edward F. Fry *et al., On the Future of Art:* Sponsored by The Solomon R. Guggenheim Museum, New York (New York: *Viking,* 1970), p. 132.

28. Rudolf Arnheim, 'The artist conscious and subconscious," *Art News* (Summer, 1957), p. 33.

29. Wassily Kandinsky, *Concerning the Spiritual in Art,* Documents of Modern Art (New York: Wittenborn, Schultz, 1947), p. 24.

30. Giorgio de Chirico, as quoted by Robert Goldwater, *Artists on Art* (New York: Pantheon, 1945), p. 440.

31. This argument was greatly assisted by an unpublished manuscript by Jacob Landau, entitled 'The Problem of Meaning in Art."

32. Ad Reinhardt, from "Twelve Rules for a New Academy," in Gregory Battcock, ed., *The New Art: A Critical Anthology* (New York: E. P. Dutton, 1966), p. 200.

33. For a discussion of the formalism found in radical realism see, for example, "Unconventional Realists," by Gabriel Laderman, *Artforum* (November, 1962).

34. Clement Greenberg, "Abstract Art," *The Nation* (April 15, 1944), p. 451.

35. Udo Kultermann, *The New Painting* (New York: Praeger, 1969), p. 60.

36. Marcel Duchamp, as quoted by Samuel Adams Greene, "Andy Warhol," in Battcock, *The New Art,* pp. 229–30.

37. Lucie-Smith, *Late Modern,* p. 9.

38. *Ibid.,* p. 272.

39. Suzanne K. Langer, *Philosophy in a New Key* (Cambridge: Harvard University, 1963), p. 57.

40. *Ibid.,* p. 60.

41. Herbert R. Kohl, *Teaching the "Unteachable"* (New York: The New York Review, 1967), p. 47.

42. Mark Rothko, "The Romantics Were Prompted," *Possibilities 1* (Winter, 1947–48), p. 84.

43. Clark, "The Blot and the Diagram," *Encounter* (January, 1963), p. 36.

44. Lawrence Alloway, "Art," *The Nation* (December 9, 1968), p. 637.

45. I would like it to be understood that my categories are designed to articulate the various ways the Humanist intention is realized. They are not intended to mean that an artist creates only one kind of Humanist art. Many of the artists presented in this book assume several stances toward the contemporary crisis, and create works that take in a number of categories.

46. Leonard Baskin, as quoted by Dale Roylance, in "Introduction" to the exhibition catalogue, *Leonard Baskin: The Graphic Work 1950–1970* (New York: Far Gallery, 1970).

47. Sigmund Abeles, in a letter to the author, 1971.

48. All quotations from "George Segal," Phyl-

lis Tuchman, *Art International* (September, 1968), p. 51.

49. Gaston Orellana, in a statement written to the author, May, 1971.
50. Manuel Ayaso, as quoted in "Art—Sensitive Spaniard," *Readers and Writers* (May–June, 1966), p. 19.
51. Statement by the artist, New York, June, 1971.
52. Carroll Greene, "Romare Bearden: The Prevalence of Ritual," *Romare Bearden: The Prevalence of Ritual* (exhibition catalogue, New York: Museum of Modern Art, 1971), p. 4.
53. Lester Johnson, as quoted in the exhibition catalogue, *The Human Situation: Street Scene 1969–1971* (New York: Martha Jackson Gallery, 1971).
54. Michael Fauerbach, as quoted in the Rhino Horn exhibition catalogue (New

York: The New School for Social Research, 1970), p. 12.
55. From an interview with Herbert Marcuse, by Lee Dembart, *New York Post* (April 28, 1971), p. 43.
56. From an unpublished interview with the artists by Cindy Nemser, 1972.
57. David L. Shirey, *New York Times* (February 13, 1971), p. 23.
58. "Each in His Own Way," the catalogue of The Commemorative Art Collection of The Florists' Transworld Delivery Association, Detroit.
59. Clement Greenberg.
60. Alice Neel, quoted in 'Artists on their Art," *Art International* (May 15, 1968) p. 48.
61. Melvin Zabarsky, in a statement written to the author, May, 1971.
62. Philip Sherrod, in an interview with the author, September, 1971.

BIBLIOGRAPHY

Books

Andrews, Benny, and Rudolf Baranik, eds. *The Attica Book.* New York: Writers' and Artists' Protest, 1973.

The ART Gallery Magazine: Second Afro-American Issue. New York: April, 1970.

Battcock, Gregory, ed. *The New Art: A Critical Anthology.* New York: E. P. Dutton, 1966.

Bell, Clive. *Art.* New York: Capricorn, 1958.

Blesh, Rudi, and Harriet Janis, eds. *de Kooning.* New York: Grove, 1960.

Cassou, Jean et al. *Art and Confrontation: The Arts in an Age of Change.* Greenwich: New York Graphic Society, 1968.

De Micheli, Mario. *Arte Contro: 1945–1970—dal realismo alla contestazione.* Milano: Vangelista Editore, 1970.

Finkelstein, Sidney. *Realism in Art.* New York: International Publishers, 1954.

Fischer, Ernst. *The Necessity of Art: A Marxist Approach.* Middlesex: Penguin, 1963.

Hess, Thomas B., and John Ashberry, eds. *Narrative Art: Art News Annual XXXVI.* New York: Macmillan, 1970.

Kahler, Erich. *The Disintegration of Form in the Arts.* New York: George Braziller, 1968.

Kirby, Michael. *Art of Our Time: Essays on the Avant-Garde.* New York: E. P. Dutton, 1969.

Knight, Everett. *The Objective Society.* New York: George Braziller, 1960.

Kohl, Herbert K. *Teaching the Unteachable.* New York: New York Review, 1967.

Langer, Suzanne K. *Philosophy in a New Key.* Cambridge: Harvard University, 1963.

————, ed. *Reflections on Art.* New York: Oxford University Press, 1961.

Lee, Rensselaer W. *Ut Pictura Poesis: The Humanistic Theory of Painting.* New York: W. W. Norton, 1967.

Lucie-Smith, Edward. *Late Modern: The Visual Arts Since 1945.* New York: Praeger, 1969.

Marcuse, Herbert. "Art as a Form of Reality." In Edward F. Fry et al. *On the Future of Art.* Sponsored by The Solomon R. Guggenheim Museum. New York: Viking, 1970.

———— *Negations.* Boston: Beacon, 1968.

———— *One Dimensional Man.* London: Sphere, 1968.

Meisel, Victor H., ed. *Voices of German Expressionism.* Englewood Cliffs: Prentice-Hall, 1970.

Morgan, George W. *The Human Predicament: Dissolution and Wholeness.* New York: Dell, 1970.

Neumeyer, Alfred. *The Search for Meaning in Modern Art.* Translated by Ruth Angress. Englewood Cliffs: Prentice-Hall, 1964.

Panofsky, Erwin. *Meaning in the Visual Arts.* Garden City: Doubleday, 1955.

Pellegrini, Aldo. *New Tendencies in Art.* New York: Crown, 1966.

Poggioli, Renato. *The Theory of the Avant-Garde.* Translated by Gerald Fitzgerald. New York: Harper & Row, 1968.

Protter, Eric, ed. *Painters on Painting.* New York: Grosset and Dunlap, 1963.

Read, Herbert. *Art and Alienation: The Role of the Artist in Society.* New York: Horizon, 1967.

———— *The Grass Roots of Art: Four Lectures on Social Aspects of Art in an Industrial Age.* Problems in Contemporary Art, Number 2. New York: Wittenborn, Schultz, 1949.

———— *Icon and Idea.* New York: Schocken, 1965.

———— *The Meaning of Art.* New York: Praeger, 1972.

Rodman, Selden. *Conversations with Artists.* New York: Capricorn, 1961.

———— *The Eye of Man: Form and Content in Western Painting.* New York: Devin-Adair, 1955.

———— *The Insiders—Rejection and Rediscovery of Man in the Arts of Our Time.* Louisiana State Press, 1960.

Rosenberg, Harold. *The Anxious Object: Art Today and Its Audience.* New York: Mentor, 1964.

———— *Artworks and Packages.* New York: Horizon, 1969.

———— *The Tradition of the New.* New York: McGraw–Hill, 1965.

Sandler, Irving. *The Triumph of American Painting: A History of Abstract Expressionism.* New York: Praeger, 1970.

Sartre, Jean-Paul. *Essays in Aesthetics.* New York: Citadel, 1963.

Shahn, Ben. *The Shape of Content.* New York: Random House, 1957.

Sontag, Susan. *Against Interpretation.* New York: Dell, 1969.

Sypher, Wylie. *Loss of the Self in Modern Literature and Art.* New York: Random House, 1964.

———— *Rococo to Cubism in Art and Literature.* New York: Random House, 1960.

Taylor, Harold. *Art and the Intellect: Moral Values and the Experience of Art.* New York: Museum of Modern Art, 1960.

Waddington, L. H. *Behind Appearance: A Study of the Relationship Between Painting and* the *Natural Sciences in This Century.* Cambridge: The MIT Press, 1969.

Whitford, Frank. *Expressionism.* London: Hamlyn, 1970.

Wimsatt, W. K. *The Verbal Icon.* University of Kentucky Press, 1954.

Wind, Edgar. *Art and Anarchy.* New York: Vintage, 1969.

Articles

Alloway, Lawrence. "Art," *The Nation* (December 9, 1968). (On Francis Bacon.)

"Art: Beyond Nightmare," *Time* (June 13, 1969). (On Miriam Beerman, Gregory Gillespie, Nancy Grossman, Paul Thek.)

"Art: The Reappearing Figure," *Time* (May 25, 1962).

"Artists on Their Art," *Art International* (May 15, 1968). (Statement by Alice Neel.)

Baro, Gene. "The Ethics of Risk," *Arts* (January, 1966).

Canaday, John. "Intruder in the Hothouse," *The New York Times* (February 7, 1971). (On Red Grooms.)

Castillejo, Jose L. "Photographic Realism: On the Paintings of Juan Genoves," *Art International* (Summer, 1966).

Cerni, Vicente Aguilera, "Reality and Silence: Rafael Canogar Today," *Art International* (Summer, 1966).

Clark, Kenneth. "The Blot and the Diagram," *Encounter* (January, 1963).

Davis, Douglas. "Monsters of Chicago," *Newsweek* (June 21, 1972). (On the Chicago Imagist Art Show.)

Dembart, Lee. "Interview with Herbert Marcuse," *New York Post* (April 28, 1971).

Gold, Barbara. " 'Human Concern/Personal Torment' Review," *Arts* (November, 1969).

Greenberg, Clement. "Abstract Art," *The Nation* (April 15, 1944).

Greene, Balcomb. "The Art of Regimentation," *South Atlantic Quarterly* (Summer, 1962).

Henry, Gerrit. "The Soho Body Snatcher," *Art News* (March, 1972). (On Duane Hanson.)

Hughes, Robert. "Dürer: Humanist, Mystic and Tourist," *Time International* (July 12, 1971).

Johnston, Richard J. H. "Students' Controversial Mural Is Obliterated at Paramus," *The New York Times* (March 28, 1971).

Kahler, Erich. "Artistic Form and the Human Condition," *University: A Princeton Quarterly* (Winter, 1967–68).

Kay, Jane Holtz. "Artists As Social Reformers," *Art in America* (January–February, 1969).

Kind, Joshua. "The Unknown Grosz," *Studio International* (March, 1967).

Laderman, Gabriel. "Unconventional Realists," *Artforum* (November, 1962).

Landau, Jacob. "Yes—No, Art—Technology," *Wilson Library Bulletin* (September, 1966).

Lester, Elenore. "The Final Decline and Total Collapse of the American Avant-Garde," *Esquire* (May, 1969).

Marcuse, Herbert. "Art in the One-Dimensional Society," *Arts* (May, 1967).

Melville, Robert, and Roland Penrose. "The Obsessive Image 1960–1968," *Art and Artists* (February, 1968).

Nemser, Cindy. "An Interview with May Stevens," *Feminist Art Journal* (September, 1972).

O'Doherty, Brian. "Leonard Baskin," *Art in America* (1963).

Peppiatt, Michael. "Francis Bacon," *Art International,* (December 20, 1968).

Perrault, John. "Tosun Bayrak: The Scourge of SoHo," *Village Voice* (October 14, 1971).

Pincus-Witten, Robert. "Peter Passuntino: Sonraed Gallery," *Artforum* (March, 1971).

"Portrait of the Artist As a Wet Hen," *Esquire* (April, 1970). (Quotes and photographs of the work of artists in the Human Concern/ Personal Torment exhibition.)

Read, Herbert. "The Necessity of Art," *Saturday Review* (September 6, 1969).

Rigg, Margaret. "Barbara Lekberg: Sculptor," *Motive* (April, 1961).

Rose, Barbara. "Oldenburg Joins the Revolution." *New York* (June 2, 1969).

Rosenberg, Harold. "The Art World: Art's Other Self," *New Yorker* (June 12, 1971).

Sandler, Irving. "An Interview with Rudolf Baranik." Unpublished.

Schjeldahl, Peter. "A World of Raucous, Challenging Images," *The New York Times* (March 22, 1970). (On the Rhino Horn show at the New School.)

Schwartz, Barry. "Art Confrontation: The Sacred Against the Profane," *Arts in Society* (Spring-Summer, 1972).

———— "The Communications Revolution: Lower Rates for Long Distance Telephone Calls or The Transformation of Society," *Arts in Society* (Summer-Fall, 1972).

———— "The Metropolitan Museum of Art: Cultural Power in a Time of Crisis," *The Metropolitan Museum of Art Bulletin* (January, 1969).

———— "Museums: Art for Who's Sake?" *Ramparts* (June, 1971).

Schwartz, Therese. "The Politicalization of the Avant-Garde," Parts I and II, *Art in America* (November–December, 1971; March–April, 1972).

Shahn, Ben. "Imagination and Intention," *Review of Existential Psychology and Psychiatry* (1967).

Skelton, Robin. "The Imagination of Jack Coughlin," *The Malahat Review* (July, 1968).

—— Foreword, "Jack Coughlin: Irish Portraits," *The Malahat Review* (April, 1972).

Stewart, William. "Humanism and Inquiry into Art Education," *Art Education* (March, 1971).

Tuchman, Phyllis. "George Segal," *Art International* (September, 1968).

Willard, Charlotte. "Violence and Art," *Art in America* (January-February, 1969).

Wilson, William. "Paul Thek: Love-Death," *Art and Artists* (April, 1968).

Exhibition Catalogues

Eduardo Arroyo: 30 Jahre danach: 30 Ans Apres. Musee d'Art Moderne de la Ville de Paris, Frankfurter Kunstverein, 1971. Foreword by Gerald Gassiot-Talbot.

Chicago Imagist Art. Museum of Contemporary Art, Chicago, 1972. Essay by Franz Schulze.

Contemporary Graphic Art on Contemporary Law and Justice. Pratt Graphics Center, Pratt Institute, New York, 1970.

Cuevas. Universidad Nacional Autonoma de Mexico, 1970. "El Mundo de Cuevas" by Fernando Benitez.

Each in His Own Way. The Commemorative Art Collection of the Florists' Transworld Delivery Association, Detroit. Text by Jan van der Marck.

Philip Evergood: Paintings and Drawings. Kennedy Galleries, New York City, 1972.

Philip Evergood. Whitney Museum of American Art, New York, 1960. Text by I. H. Baur.

Five German Printmakers. Associated American Artists Gallery, New York, 1971. (Reiner Schwarz is included in this exhibition.)

Funk. University Art Museum, Berkeley, California, 1967. Text by Peter Selz.

Gropper. A.C.A. Galleries, New York, 1970. Text by George Albert Perret.

Chaim Gross—Sculptures. Forum Gallery, New York City, 1967.

Human Concern/Personal Torment: The Grotesque in American Art. Whitney Museum of American Art, New York, 1969. Text by Robert Doty.

The Humanist Tradition in Contemporary American Painting. New School Art Center, New York, 1968.

Jonah Kinigstein. A.C.A. Galleries, New York, 1966.

Jacob Landau: Woodcuts and Lithographs. As-sociated American Artists Gallery, New York, 1970. Essay by Alan Fern.

Jack Levine: Recent Paintings. Kennedy Galleries, New York, 1972. "A Painter of Modern Life," by Mahonri Sharp Young.

Antonio Lopez-Garcia. Staempfli Gallery, New York, 1968.

Giacomo Manzu: The Touchstone Suite. FAR Gallery, New York, 1970. Text by Herman J. Wechsler.

Maryan: New Paintings. Allen Frumkin Gallery, New York, 1969.

"The Nazi Drawings" by Mauricio Lasansky. Mauricio Lasansky Foundation, 1966. Essay by Edwin Honig. (Published in conjunction with several exhibitions of the Nazi Drawings.)

New Images of Man. Museum of Modern Art, New York, 1959. Text by Peter Selz.

1969: Twelve Afro-American Artists. Lee Nordness Galleries, New York. Essay by Carroll Greene.

The Obsessive Image 1960–1968. Institute of Contemporary Arts, London, 1968. Essay by Mario Amaya.

Elliot Offner. Forum Gallery, New York, 1964.

Orellana. Galleria Schubert, Milan, 1971.

Protest and Hope. New School Art Center, New York, 1967. Foreword by Paul Mocsanyi.

Joyce Reopel. Cober Gallery, New York, 1965.

Rhino Horn. The New School for Social Research, New York, 1970. Introduction by D. Stephen Pepper.

Ben Shahn. Kennedy Galleries, New York, 1968. Essay by Frank Getlein.

Sidney Simon: Mirror Series. Graham Gallery, New York, 1971.

Three Artists View the Human Condition: Jacob Landau, Stefan Martin, Gregori Prestopino. New Jersey State Museum, Trenton, 1968.

Venice 34: The Figurative Tradition in Recent American Art. The Smithsonian Institution Press, Washington, D.C., 1968. Selected by Norman A. Geske.

Weimar—Nurnberg—Bonn: An Exhibition of German Posters—Art as a Political Weapon. The Art Center of the New School for Social Research, New York, 1963. Text by Paul Mocsanyi.

Young Mexicans. Art Gallery for the Center for Inter-American Relations, New York, 1971. Essay by Jacqueline Barnitz. (Francisco Corzas is included.)

INDEX

Page numbers in italics refer to illustrations.

PHOTO CREDITS

Christina O. Ben-Yehuda
Anthony J. Bruder
Geoffrey Clements
Vivian Crozier
Bevan Davies
Jonas Davydenas
Leonard Horowitz
Eric Leong
Master Institute of United Arts
Materna Studio

O. E. Nelson
Edward Peterson
Philadelphia Museum of Art
Eric Pollitzer
Nathan Rabin
Walter Rosenblum
Walter Russell
John D. Schiff
Schopplein Studio
Scott Studio

Warren E. Straw III
Betsy Swanson
Swicord and Associates
Frank J. Thomas
Edward Trieber
Crispin Vazquez
Susan Weiley
Ralph Weiss